DEATH
and
LIFE
An American Theology

DEATH
and
LIFE

An American Theology

Arthur C. McGill

Edited and with an
Afterword by Charles A. Wilson
and Per M. Anderson

FORTRESS PRESS   PHILADELPHIA

Library of Congress Cataloging-in-Publication Data

McGill, Arthur Chute.
  Death and life.

  1. Death—Religious aspects—Christianity. 2. Death—
Social aspects—United States. 3. Jesus Christ—
Person and offices. I. Anderson, Per M. II. Wilson,
Charles A. (Charles Alan), 1947-   III. Title.
BT825.M36 1987   236'.1   86-45215
ISBN 0-8006-1927-7

2548F86   Printed in the United States of America   1-1927

Contents

Acknowledgments

This book is a posthumous reconstruction of a set of lectures given by Arthur C. McGill at the St. Olaf College Summer Theological Conference. For three days in 1974 McGill engaged and disoriented an audience of pastors and their spouses. The transformation of speech into the written word cannot fully preserve the powerful event of voice. As editors, however, we have taken pains to render the lectures worthy of reading. But we have not disguised their oral flavor. McGill's disorienting word remains. The text, in fact, is deliberately open-ended; it invites rereading and reconsideration.

Lucille McGill and her children kindly gave us permission to proceed with the project and provided us a partial handwritten copy of the original lectures. We wish to thank President Emeritus Harlan F. Foss and St. Olaf College for financial support. Arthur T. Droge, Langdon B. Gilkey, and James M. Gustafson of the University of Chicago have read and advised us on the manuscript. Paul Ramsey of Princeton University and William F. May of Southern Methodist University have also aided us in the research. Harold H. Ditmanson, Edmund N. Santurri, and Gary Stansell of the St. Olaf Religion Department provided us with helpful advice and support, and WCAL–AM and FM, public radio at St. Olaf College, provided us with the tapes of the lectures.

Per M. Anderson
Charles A. Wilson

Introduction

I have always been struck by the extraordinary contrast between the attitudes toward death found everywhere in our society and the attitudes toward death exhibited by Jesus as he is presented in the New Testament. This contrast is deep and fascinating and disturbing. Not the least perplexing feature of the situation is the fact that the Christian churches in the United States often seem to be better teachers of this society's view of death than of Jesus' view.

I will try to exhibit what I see to be this remarkable contrast, and this task determines the sequence of my topics. In chapters 1 and 2 I will describe what I think are some of the attitudes toward death that pervade our lives in the United States. I do not believe any individual, much less any community, ever has one single attitude toward the mystery of death. I shall describe two connected strands that are rather prevalent in our country. In chapters 3, 4, and 5 I consider three different aspects of how, through the New Testament writings, death appears in the light of Jesus Christ. From the beginning, however, we must be clear about the fact that the word "death" can be used with a narrow and with a broad meaning.

In the narrow sense, death refers simply to that moment, that instant when life ends. It is that terminal point. Today, there are extensive discussions in the medical profession about what symptoms should be taken as signaling this end of life, the instant of death. For the sake of heart transplants, surgeons must be certain that the donors are dead before removing their hearts. Otherwise, they would be removing the heart of a living person and thereby would become responsible for that person's death. If we consider death in this narrow sense as the instant when life ends, a very important consequence follows. As long as we live, death is something future. It is an event out ahead of us. As long as we are, then there is no death. And when there is death, we no longer are.

What kind of knowledge can we have of death, if death is identified as some future end of our life? How can we know about it, and how can we discover when to expect it? When death is identified simply with the instant that life ends, it is treated as that which is known by observation, that is, in terms of the disappearance of those bodily activities which are taken to be the vital signs of life. Death is known when the breathing stops, when the heartbeat stops, when certain patterns of the encephalograph cease to register. Death here becomes accessible primarily as an empirical event. Like all empirical events, it requires experts to observe it, and these experts are the physicians. Therefore, in order for anyone to know about his or her death in this narrow sense of the term, to know about the approaching instant of the end of life, he or she must be informed by the doctor. Even if personally he or she feels awful, even if he or she senses from within that life is ending, that kind of knowledge is not relevant.

As the end of life, death always belongs to the realm of observational data. To know it in this regard, we must wait for the doctor to say, "I'm afraid I have bad news for you. . . ." In short, *death in this narrow sense is known primarily by other people.* I call this way of identifying death the *medical viewpoint.* Death is a future event of our visible nature, out ahead of us somewhere. We rely on the medical profession to tell us when it is approaching (the patient is on "the critical list") or when it is imminent or unavoidable (the patient's condition is now "terminal"). Elisabeth Kübler-Ross, in her book *On Death and Dying*, deals with death entirely in terms of this medical viewpoint.[1] Death is considered entirely as a terminal event. Death happens to a person at the very end of life. Kübler-Ross is interested in the attitudes of people toward their dying. Does she consider how they have thought of the little deaths they have known throughout their lives? Not at all. Death is exclusively the medical event of cessation of life. As such, no one can have any relation to it until a physician has determined empirically that death is near. Only then, for Kübler-Ross, do people have attitudes toward death that merit examination. According to this medical view of death no one has a real relation to death until there is medical evidence to show that life is ending.

There is, however, a second and much larger way of using the word "death." Here death is not only, and perhaps not primarily, the instant when life finally ends. Rather death refers to all the gradual and recurrent experiences where life is known to be failing. Death is not so much the final instant when life terminates as it is the process which leads up to and culminates in that instant. We should perhaps say "dying" rather than death. Death is not known empirically by someone else who observes us and tells us what to expect according to the laws of some segment of nature. This death is known only from within, by the person who lives. It is apprehended as the failure or the collapse or the slowing down of that vitality, that energy and potency which characterize the experience of life.

In the broad sense, death is not some future event observable primarily by someone else. Death is going on within us all the time. Every time we are sick we hear from within what death shall mean to us personally. Illness is a foretaste of death; it is the concrete experience where each of us discovers how our own existence becomes impossible. Every separation from a loved one is a foretaste of death. Each evening, every letting go of the conscious world in sleep is a foretaste of death: "Now I lay me down to sleep, I pray; if I should die before I wake, I pray." The connection of sleep and death is deep and real. From this perspective, death is not some future objective event about which we can be forewarned by our physicians. *Death is the losing of life, that wearing away which goes on all the time.*

Each new period of life we enter represents the loss forever—the death—of that previous period. In adolescence our childhood is forever dead. In middle age our early adulthood is forever dead. Each year marks more of life that we have lost. A person may say proudly, "I am forty," to show how much he or she has lived. The fool! "Forty" marks the number of years of his or her life that have been taken away. It marks the measure of his or her loss: the possibilities of joy or love or development that never bear fruit; the biophysical deterioration that, at some levels, begins even before we are born, while we are still in our mothers' wombs; the constant wear that belongs essentially to every moment of living experience. These diminutions of life constitute this broader meaning of the word death.

"We don't die for one second out there in the future, we die all the time, in every direction. Every meal we eat breaks down the enamel."[2] We are continually taking leave, continually parting and looking towards the end; we are continually disappointed, ceaselessly piercing through realities into their nothingness; we continually exclude ourselves from many rich possibilities of life by our actual decisions. In what we constantly do in the course of our daily lives, we are dying.

In what follows I am not particularly interested in the instant of death; that is, I am not interested in the medical viewpoint which treats death as some special moment. I do not think that the isolated instant has much importance. More important is our own immediate, ongoing experience of the failure of life. That is the death which we know continually. That is the death which we try to understand with stories and myths. Only with such stories can we body forth the character of final death. From this perspective final death does not stand as the externally known instant when all the observable signs of life disappear from the body's appearances. From this perspective, final death is simply the end point of the process of disintegration which goes on continually. In fact, Augustine even claimed that death, in the medical sense, is actually the end of real death, the end of this dying process in our lives, the end of our experience of dying.[3] Michael Fraenkel writes, "We never know Death. We know only the little deaths we die as our years fall from us, leaving their work of sundering and separation . . . the hurt and pain: the scar."[4] I believe, however, that we all secure our sense of what final death may mean by projecting and expanding, even maximizing our experiences of these little deaths.

NOTES

1. Elisabeth Kübler-Ross, *On Death and Dying* (New York: Macmillan, 1969).
2. John Updike, *Couples* (New York: Alfred A. Knopf, 1968), 370.
3. Augustine, *The City of God* 13.10.
4. Quoted in Joseph C. Rheingold, *The Mother, Anxiety and Death: The Catastrophic Death Complex* (Boston: Little, Brown & Co., 1967), 14.

1

The American Worship of Death:
Ethics

Americans like to appear as if they give death hardly any thought at all. Of course, death will happen to all of us someday, but until then, it is not something to think about or grapple with. Until then our preoccupation should be with life and with all of its challenges and adventures. Let the dying deal with death. Our calling is to enjoy life. In this regard the *popular* view and what I have just called the *medical* view of death are essentially alike, although as I shall try to show, they are based on very different convictions. Both think of death as something future, normally as something remote and hypothetical—not as something that hangs over and works within every present moment of life.

This way of thinking about death is the attitude to which people refer when they speak of American optimism. Let me emphasize how broadly and deeply optimism runs in the fabric of American life. Because of their *neediness*, human beings have always been victimized.[1] They have been victimized by other individuals or by social institutions, by nature or by circumstances beyond human control (by what are legally known as "acts of God"): a child is born mentally retarded; a young woman is disfigured by fire; a nation of millions suffers prolonged drought with devastating famine. In their normal response to these threats, people try to acquire something, some knowledge or resource, that will protect them from this deprivation. They may develop plastic surgery for burned faces or a water storage and irrigation system for drought. They try to defend themselves against the slings and arrows of fortune by securing something in their control, in their possession, or in their being, which will save and restore them in the face of every danger. I call this response to disaster the *technique of having*, since it is by having available some object or some skill or some resource that people may cope with a threatening evil.[2]

THE TECHNIQUE OF HAVING

For most societies such having is no more than an impossible hope or a matter of unexpected good fortune. In the United States, however, successful having is often taken as a fact. You know the expression, "We are the richest nation in the world; how can we have poverty?" Consider the statement carefully. It states two facts: first, the United States is the richest nation in the world; and second, there is poverty here. But notice how it interprets these two facts. By its tone and style the statement gives the impression that in a country like the United States poverty should not exist. It thus attaches a very different importance to these two facts. It expresses surprise that there is poverty. The second fact is taken as unexpected. In other words, it looks upon richness and wealth as the true, the basic, the essential, and controlling condition of life in the United States. It reflects the belief that American initiative or American know-how, American technology or American unselfishness is such that we in this country can really remove all poverty, all misery, and all suffering. And if these evils are not yet actually removed, their continuing presence is judged to be somehow accidental. They no longer belong to the inner and inescapable fabric of life. If they occur, it is because something went wrong. Some fluke happened, and the normal adequacy of our skills and resources, the fullness of our life, momentarily failed. Normally and properly, life in the United States is a matter of all people having enough to satisfy them and protect them. Poverty and inadequacy, those foretastes of death, are abnormal conditions. We are the richest nation in the world; how can *we* have poverty?

Once we identify this attitude, we can easily see it running deeply throughout American life. Listen to Americans greet each other. At a party close your eyes and concentrate carefully on the tones of voice. "How are you?" "Fine . . . fine . . . fine." The question and answer are always optimistic, always affirmative. They are, in fact, preliminary social reminders that we are permitted to deal with one another only in terms of an assurance that we are free from all unanswered needs. We are expected, preliminarily anyway, to relate to one another only with the assurance that our pains and inadequacies, that the shadows of death in us are no more than passing accidents, that each of us already possesses resources for every contingency.

Look at the aims of our entire educational effort in the United States. One single philosophy seems to dominate all others: the belief that everyone should become all that he or she is capable of being, that he or she should realize full capacities, should expand to his or her full growth, and should show himself or herself finally in proper shape and stature. Education functions to help all Americans to develop the *wealth* within their personal selves, and thus to help them make their own rich contribution to our common life. Courtship and marriage are usually conceived in the same way. As the phrase goes, we must "attract" someone—which means having such personal richness and so packaging and displaying it, that someone of the other sex will respond. Courtship, like everything else, becomes a matter of displaying and exchanging available wealth.

Look at the moral development of American children. No American child is taught: "You will constantly find yourself with needs that cannot be satisfied, with destructive circumstances that cannot be controlled. Therefore, learn courage and endurance to bear needs and in need learn how to receive and how to give. Learn not to be emotionally overthrown by unrelieved pain and unforeseen disaster." Not a moment is wasted teaching such negative virtues to American children. On the contrary, unanswered need is only an abnormal accident. No one prepares for it; everyone prepares to run away from it. American children are morally developed with those virtues that help them to acquire some kind of richness. If they have ambition, self-confidence, a willingness to work (oh, a willingness to work!), a tolerance of routine, a capacity for putting off their immediate satisfactions, and a devotion to long-range goals, then they will get ahead. Then they will be in a position to secure the resources necessary to handle all their needs and disasters.

In the United States, then, wealth is not just a fact. It is a state of mind. It is a central and taproot value. At point after point in our daily lives we show how convinced we are that we have solved the problems of human existence by the technique of having: by encouraging individual freedom; by giving a talent-oriented education; by seeking out the natural resources in every continent; by exploiting those resources with the full productive power of technology; and by training people not to accept their deficiencies but to secure a variety of riches for every need. The American way of life has been marked by extraordinary confidence. Therefore, we should really not speak of a technique of having, but of a *gospel of having.* Gospel means good news, and for much of America wealth is the good news that will save and redeem us from all evil: the wealth of money, the wealth of scientific knowledge, the wealth of social diversity, the wealth of individual opportunity, the wealth of military power, the wealth of international prestige, the wealth of God's unreserved goodness to us—America the beautiful, toward which all history moves!

Such is the character of what I am calling American optimism. Because of the riches of nature when exploited by the ingenuity of the mind, because of the riches of the human personality, life can be happy, satisfying, and good. Sickness, poverty, and injustice can be removed, provided we work on these problems hard enough and long enough. This optimism is beautifully reflected in an advertisement seeking contributions for the United Negro College Fund. "People are born every day," declares the ad, "who could cure disease, make peace, create art, abolish injustice and hunger, but they will never get a chance to do those things without an education." That is to say: With a little better effort in doing what we have been doing all along, we shall make peace, abolish injustice, end hunger, cure sickness. In short, we shall remove all the negatives of life and all the foretastes of death.

AMERICAN OPTIMISM:
DEATH OUTSIDE OF LIFE

What is the character of death, then, as seen by this American optimism? First and most important, death is thought of as something wholly outside of life and unrelated to life. Life is what is normal. Death is something that intrudes from outside. It befalls us. There is nothing in life itself, according to this view, that makes death necessary or essential. Life is not sustained by the death and eating of other life. My goodness no—that's not American! In America life is nourished with no real dying at all. Or again, the life of all is not sustained by everyone cutting down their standard of living, consuming less, eating less, surrendering comforts and forgoing some basic satisfactions so that all may have a little nourishment. My goodness no—that's not American! In America, people can consume everything they possibly can, as rapidly as they possibly can, and there will still be more than enough for everyone. In short, to use the American word, death is always accidental. It has no real basis in life. It does not belong to life.

Now, to speak in this way is to speak in purely formal terms. There is also a very important value aspect entailed in this viewpoint. What does it really mean to say that death is outside of life, that it has no basis in life, no essential connection with life? What does it mean to say that death gives no crucial service to life and is purely accidental? Motivationally and ethically, it means that all human beings should devote themselves exclusively to life, for here lies all value and all meaning and all good. Furthermore, one should have no truck with death. Death should never be part of the aims and aspirations of any human being. In other words, death is so totally outside of life, that it is also totally outside of human aspirations and value. No one should seek death or exalt death or give any significance to death. It is totally anti-human. Arnold Zweig has expressed this sense, "death was like an idiot, who split a violin for firewood and used it to heat the stove."[3] This sense of death is bodied forth in the idea of death as extermination. Death is obliteration of everything human.

On this basis ethicist Paul Ramsey rejects the idea of death with dignity. Death is oblivion and nothingness. It deprives people of everything making for worth in this, their world. It is in fact the end of all worth because it is the end of a person, for whom and from whom all worth has its reality. Therefore, we should never try to prettify death or dignify death. As the negation of life, death is only a gross indignity.[4] Ramsey thus gives expression to the ethical aspect of the American conviction that death is outside of life. This means that death is outside of all value and all meaning, because for Americans value and meaning belong exclusively to life. For anyone to accept death or dignify death would be to deny human value and dignity. Death is the total enemy.

We are now in a position to understand how the popular view of death as outside of life differs from the medical view, which also sees death as outside of life. When physicians treat death as an observable cessation of life processes, they are simply following the assumptions of the biologist. They hold to a viewpoint of a technical science which has been developed in the interest of the scientific explanation of nature. When physicians say that death is outside of life, they are talking about the objective world as it exists out there, independent of us. But the popular view is not a matter of science, not a matter of understanding what is there in the world, already given to us. The popular view is concerned with motivations and aspirations. For ordinary people, life is not a given phenomenon to be understood scientifically. Life is a task and an adventure to be willed, executed, and actualized. When ordinary people feel that death is outside of life, they are thinking of life as that which we must bring about by living correctly.

Consider how this popular American view of death (as outside of all life and as the negation of all value) helps to shape the ethical life of every American. This popular view is not the only ethical influence, but it is one very important influence. What is the most crucial task required by this viewpoint? The most crucial task is for people to create a living world where death seems abnormal and accidental. They must create a living world where life is so full, so secure, and so rich with possibilities that it gives no hint of death and deprivation. Here we have the first ethical duty imposed by the conviction that death is outside of life and that life is the only good for which we should live. According to this duty, a person must try to live in such a way that he or she does not carry the marks of death, does not exhibit any hint of the failure of life. A person must try to prove by his or her own existence that failure does not belong essentially to life. Failure is an accident, a remediable breakdown of the system.

THE ETHIC OF AVOIDANCE

As we observe our lives in this country, we cannot help but be struck by the effort Americans make to appear to be full of life. I believe this duty is ingrained deeply in everyone. Only if we can create around us a life apparently without failure, can we convince ourselves that death is indeed outside, is indeed accidental, is indeed the unthinkable enemy. In other words, the belief that death is outside of life is not a fact to be acknowledged; it is a condition to be attained. Consider the American commitment to nice appearances. We often speak of the suburbs in terms of neat and flawless appearances. When we look at the lawns and the shrubs and the solid paint of those homes, who can believe the human misery that often goes on within them? And given the fine appearances of the suburbs, who can tolerate the slums of the inner city? After all, there we see life collapsing and going to pieces. Urban renewal is required, not to improve the living condition of the people, for they are simply moved elsewhere to less conspicuous slums. It is not to increase the tax revenue, because so much of urban renewal involves tax breaks, subsidized construction, and government office buildings. Rather, urban renewal is required in order to remove from the city that visible mark of the failure of life.

How about aging? Aging shows that debility and the loss of life belong essentially to life, that life is mortal through and through. Apparently many Americans are taught that it is shameful for us to show ourselves growing old. There are enormous industries that do nothing but help people conceal their age under some kind of youthful patina. In fact, the whole of American culture gives prominence to youth. Why? I think it is because youth is the time that is full of life, when all the negatives are only minor and accidental. Youth is the actualization, then, of the American ethic. It is to be expected that the American people, so far as they want to create a living world which seems to have no place for death, will idolize youth as the best and truest time of life, and will teach individuals to value anyone who can maintain the style and appearance of youth.

What about failure? Are Americans taught to expect failure and to maintain their dignity and equanimity in the face of failure? Certainly not. From diapers onward, every American is severely punished for failure. Failure is not an essential and inescapable element in life. Normally, societies accept the fact that failure is inherent in the human situation. If anyone continually succeeds, that has nothing to do with his or her effort. Such success is a miracle from beyond the human scene. Accepting failure, however, is not common in the United States. Failure here is a disgrace. No child is taught how to cope with it, only how to keep away from it.

What about the people who do fail in America? And what about those who collapse of life? What about the sick and the aged and the deformed and the mentally retarded? Do they not remind us that the marks of death are always working within the fabric of life? No, because in the United States, deliberately and systematically, with the force of the law itself, we compel all such people to be sequestered where we cannot see them.[5] You'll find no beggars on the streets of America. You'll visit few homes where a very aged person is present and where that person's imminent dying is integrated into the rhythm of family life. As for the insane, they are hidden in such well-landscaped institutions, behind such beautiful lawns and trees, that when we drive by in our shiny automobiles we cannot imagine the suffering that goes on within those walls.

Every American is thus ingrained with the duty to look well, to seem fine, to exclude from the fabric of his or her normal life any evidence of decay and death and helplessness. The ethic I have outlined here is often called the ethic of success. I prefer to call it the *ethic of avoidance*. Success is not the achievement of some goal; it is not success in that narrow sense of attained goals. Success here refers to a whole style of life, an array of manners and appearances: the successful marriage, the successful career, the successful neighborhood, the feeling of success. But in all this, the shadows of alien death are never far from anyone's consciousness. "You hear what happened to Mr. Jacob's father?" "The house needs painting, dear; it's beginning to crack." "John, has the insurance been paid?" "How can we get rid of all this pollution?"

Notice that success is essentially measured not so much by any ideal of extraordinary positive achievement, but rather by the degree to which the marks of decay and death are kept away. That is to say, success does not pursue the good, but seeks to flee from death. It is always looking over its shoulder at the alien enemy. The ethic of success is really an ethic of avoidance. Persons are considered a success not because they attain some remarkable goal, but because their lives do not betray marks of failure or depression, helplessness or sickness. When they are asked how they are, they really can say and really do say, "Fine . . . fine."

Success, then, is not so much a goal but a style of life. And the ethic of avoidance cuts more deeply into our lives than we often realize. Today, for instance, if a young woman expects to bear a deformed child, she may well decide to have an abortion, not because she lacks love, but because her love is instructed and guided by the ethic of avoidance. She has been taught that true life involves being free from the marks of destitution and debility. True life occurs when death is accidental. In these terms it can only seem wrong for her to bring into the world someone who will be deformed or debilitated. In having the abortion she is simply obeying the ethic of success or, better, the ethic of avoidance.

THE ETHIC OF RESISTANCE

There is, however, a second ethical duty that grows out of our American optimism. In spite of all we can do, death and the marks of death do come. People do get sick; children are born retarded; food is not given to the poor; the resources necessary for life threaten to give out. The ethic of avoidance is not enough. We must also fight against death and the marks of death whenever they appear. That is to say, we must also maintain an *ethic of resistance.* We require a police force to prevent social disorder, a medical establishment to oppose sickness, a welfare system for the impoverished.

Why is there this passion to gather people into the arena of true life and to remove from them all marks of sickness and debility? Because many Americans have to create a society which does not cause or require debility and death. Life, life, and more life—that is the only horizon within which these Americans want to live. Epidemics of sickness, economic disasters bringing mass starvation, social violence and disorder threatening at every street corner—if any such things were to happen, then death would no longer be outside of life, be accidental to life. Then, the American venture of nice homes, clean streets, decent manners, and daily security would prove to be false. Events would discredit the belief that Americans need only to devote themselves to the pursuit and enhancement of life, and need not learn those negative virtues by which other humans have always borne failure, pain, and loss. If Americans do not remove the slums with urban renewal, do not cure one disease after another, do not maintain public order and economic stability, then one important strand in the entire moral fabric of this society would be shattered. It seems to me the Vietnam War shook that fabric as nothing else had in a long time. For too many, it intimated that the highest order of national policy might move in stupid and destructive ways. Americans, too, like all other humans, might have to include within their daily horizons shame and evil and death as aspects inherent in life and not simply as accidental. Such is my understanding of one prevailing American attitude toward life and death. Death and the marks of death have no place in life. Death is totally outside, totally accidental, totally anti-human. The only possible human attitudes are avoidance and resistance.

GRATITUDE AND CHARITY

Let me emphasize the important role which Christian churches play, perhaps unwittingly, in supporting this American attitude. American Christian churches rigorously direct religious sentiment into two channels. First, American Christian churches insist on the importance of the gratitude generated by the actual life situation in which Americans find themselves. If Americans are able to devote themselves exclusively to life and more life, and can turn away from death as something accidental and anti-human, this is because of the goodness of God. It is God's doing, and consequently, American Christian churches teach their members to be grateful to God. But how are we to be grateful to God? By living for life, by enjoying life, and by striving to keep every trace of rottenness, failure, and death out of our lives.

When God's goodness is conceived as the gift to us of our good way of life, Christmas becomes the festival when this gratitude can be expressed. At Christmas people can exhibit their faithfulness to God's goodness by spending for the things of life, by enjoying the things of life, by celebrating the fullness of life. In the old Christian calendar, on December 26, the church celebrated the martyrdom of Saint Stephen and on December 28, the death of the infants whom Herod killed. Once, Christmas was embedded in suffering, in injustice, and in death. The joy of Christmas belonged precisely where these negatives were known to operate. But this is not so for many Christians in the United States. Many Christian Americans believe that they stand exclusively in life. For them, death is somehow accidental, and therefore, Christmas should be exclusively merry. Yet they also know that, for them to stand exclusively in life, they must thank God.

Second, American churches direct their members to help the unfortunate. According to this church teaching, Americans are not alone in their belief that all marks of suffering and devastation should be removed from the ordinary rhythm of life. This view, it is claimed, is also the will of Jesus. Though he lived many centuries before America was discovered, somehow Jesus was able to express the American belief that the sufficiency of the things of this world and the goodness of the motives of the human heart are adequate to take care of all human misery. Alongside the *call to gratitude*, then, American Christianity also maintains the call to resistance, that is, the *call to charity*. In short, American churches give important religious support to the two basic ethics which arise from the belief that death is outside of life. The ethic of avoidance is associated with gratitude to God. And the ethic of resistance is associated with Jesus' call to love the neighbor.

NOTES

1. For a more thorough treatment of the condition of neediness, see McGill's *Suffering: A Test of Theological Method* (Philadelphia: Westminster Press, 1982), chaps. 1 and 2.

2. The influence of Gabriel Marcel on McGill appears with the "technique of having." See Marcel's *The Philosophy of Existence*, trans. Manya Harari (London: Harvill Press, 1948), 18–19.

3. Arnold Zweig, *Education Before Verdun*, trans. Eric Sutton (New York: Viking Press, 1936), 398.

4. McGill's source for this account of Ramsey is unknown, even to Ramsey. Given McGill's critical judgment, readers are encouraged to consult Ramsey's published reflections on death. See Paul Ramsey, "The Indignity of 'Death with Dignity,'" in *Death Inside Out*, ed. Peter Steinfels and Robert M. Veatch (New York: Harper & Row, 1974), 81–96; and idem, "Death's Pedagogy," *Commonweal* (20 September 1974): 497–502.

5. See William F. May, "Institutions as Symbols of Death," *Journal of the American Academy of Religion* 42 (June 1976): 211–23.

2

The American Worship of Death:
Beliefs and Difficulties

In the first chapter I reflected upon American optimism and the widespread conviction that death is somehow outside of life, unrelated to life, and is the pure negation of life. I also distinguished between two ethical impulses which grow out of that conviction. In the first impulse people attempt to prove that death and decay are not embedded deeply in their lives. They try to live completely in terms of life, and instead of taking on and wrestling with suffering and destitution, they run away from any mark of death the instant it appears. They work to cover their whole existence in a purely affirmative style. They exude success and health. I refer to this impulse as the ethic of success because under its influence people try to believe that successful living is, or at least should be, an actual, normal, day-by-day accomplishment. I also refer to it as the ethic of avoidance because people measure their success, their fullness of life, by how free they can be from all the negatives. True life is not a matter of bearing and enduring and remaining human under the pressure of the negative. True life is a matter of avoiding the negatives altogether.

For instance, consider the case of Senator Thomas Eagleton, whom George McGovern named as his running mate during the 1972 presidential campaign. No one questioned how strong or how well he was psychologically; it was simply a fact that he had had shock treatments. He carried a mark of weakness, no matter how successfully he may have overcome it. And the sheer fact was enough to tell us all that he was not our kind of vice-president. Once my daughter and I were in Virginia where we visited

Williamsburg; I looked closely at the people there (myself included), and they were all so clean, so neat, so tanned, so buoyant and assured. I couldn't see suffering; I couldn't see fear; I couldn't see death in any of them. I can't imagine where they carry their nightmares, their savagery, their decay and madness, their grief for all the suffering in the world. On their faces and in their walks there was not a trace of such things.

In memory of my visit to Williamsburg, then, let me call those who live according to the ethic of success or avoidance the *bronze people.* They devote themselves to expunging from their lives every appearance, every intimation of death. Their lives help assure us all that death is indeed outside of us. Yet to be a bronze person, to be able to live this way and convey this impression, is not easy and is not natural. In fact, it is one of the most disciplined and strenuous moral achievements. It is a constant and all-demanding task. It must be carried out in every area of a person's life. There is no point in wearing nice clothes but having your eyes conspicuously haunted by fear. There is no point in walking and smiling with self-assured confidence if your face is deformed. All traces of weakness, debility, ugliness, and helplessness must be kept away from every part of a person's life. The task must be done every single day if such persons really are to convince us that they do not carry the smell of death within them. It takes discipline to keep one's garments cleaned and pressed, to keep the styling of one's clothes up-to-date, to keep the house painted. When a member of one's family dies, it takes discipline not to wear an armband, not to identify publicly with one's grief.

Lucy Arnaz, as a young actress, gave an interview which appeared in the *Washington Post.* "I don't know what my career will be like," she said. "I hope I'll be around approximately forever. At the moment I love my work like mad."[1] That's a statement of the pure bronze vision: enthusiastic, dedicated, succeeding, and expecting to go on approximately forever. But for a grown-up person to make a statement as idiotic as that takes concentrated self-discipline. The ethic of success and avoidance expresses the conviction that the good life is a matter of excluding all negatives, on the belief that death and its marks are indeed outside of life.

The ethic of avoidance is one important impulse. Another impulse moves people to resist the marks of death wherever they appear and to do as much as possible to remove them entirely from the lives of all people. Therefore, a war is conducted, a war against suffering, against injustice, against poverty, against sickness, against aging—in short, against all the forms of deprivation and death. That war, of course, is conducted from the vantage point of life, as if we could identify ourselves exclusively with life and could attack all these negatives as alien conditions which should not, and essentially do not, belong to our lives. It is as if their presence were unnecessary, were some kind of mistake, which sustained effort will remove. As I see it, both the ethic of avoidance and the ethic of resistance are based on the conviction that the lives we live are not essentially and intrinsically mortal.

There is a passage which captures the ethic of avoidance from Albert Camus's novel *The Plague*. The people of Oran in Algeria are becoming sick. For the first time the word "plague" is used:

> Everybody knows that pestilences have a way of recurring in the world; yet somehow we find it hard to believe in ones that crash down on our heads from a blue sky. There have been as many plagues as wars in history; yet always plagues and wars take people equally by surprise. . . . In this respect our townsfolk were like everybody else, wrapped up in themselves; in other words they were humanists; they disbelieved in pestilences. A pestilence isn't a thing made to man's measure; therefore we tell ourselves that pestilence is a mere bogy of the mind, a bad dream that will pass away. But it doesn't always pass away and, from one bad dream to another, it is men who pass away, and the humanists first of all, because they haven't taken their precautions. Our townsfolk were not more to blame than others; they forgot to be modest, that was all, and thought that everything still was possible for them; which presupposed that pestilences were impossible. They went on doing business, arranged for journeys, and formed views. How should they have given a thought to anything like plague, which rules out any future, cancels journeys, silences the exchange of views. They fancied themselves free, and no one will ever be free so long as there are pestilences.[2]

If we could replace the terms "plague" and "pestilence" with the term "death," this passage would describe perfectly the attitude embodied so vividly in the appearances and the manner of the bronze people.

DEATH AS MUTILATION

In this chapter I want to examine a very different attitude which is also prevalent. Here I am thinking of the way in which the newspapers and the television channels give us a daily dose of photographs of highway accidents and other disasters. Here we are confronted with situations that stand totally opposed to the bronze people's world. I would like especially to call attention to two aspects of the attitude which these photographs reflect. First, these photos clearly express a sense of death as the violent mutilation of human beings. We see the bloody bodies sprawled over the asphalt or crushed within the car. We see the plane wreckage, the building gutted by fire, the victims with every sort of injury and disfigurement. What we have here is not simply an artificial preoccupation with sensational events. Rather we have the use of these scenes to body forth a sense of what death is.

Death is essentially mutilation, the catastrophic mutilation of the human, embodied person.[3] Of course, death does not always impose such visible mutilation as may occur in the plane crash or the auto accident. But when we see someone brutally broken on the highway, we read this as making visible what death does essentially, always, and to everyone. Death breaks into the integrity of a person's biophysical, psychosocial system. Death violates and mangles that life system. Even when it only appears to cause a person to weaken slowly, death involves severe violence being done to the human spirit and the human organism: muscles quiver; breathing is labored; the integrity of the life process is being shattered. An automobile accident simply presents this real work of death in a visibly outrageous way.

Our manner of representing death, then, conveys one thing very decisively: it shows that death entails some kind of distorting and destructive activity, some kind of active violence being done to the life system which normally works smoothly or well. Death here is not the cessation of life, not the lowering of the fires; *it is being killed.* It is the work of some obscure agency or power that violently smashes or subtly insinuates itself into a person's network of life-support processes. Whether death is caused by disease or sickness, by accident or old age, it is imaged forth as active violation. In the study of religions a term is used to designate the belief that disaster and death represent the working of some kind of destructive activity or agency. Such a viewpoint is called a belief in the *demonic.* Today in the United States there is a widespread tendency to experience and to image death in a demonic way. Some destructive agency intrudes into and mutilates what normally sustains us in life.[4]

A second feature about the coverage of death in the media sets it even more fully opposed to the bronze people's vision of life. The news reports have a way of making every disaster seem unexpected. It is as if the marks of death erupt into life just when we least expect it, just when we think we have taken all our precautions. Who can defend themselves against the careless or drunken driver, against the irrational killer who shoots from a university tower in Austin, Texas or from a pew in an Atlanta church? Who can be sure that their new car may not be one that should be recalled by the maker because of a faulty steering wheel? Because of the energy crisis, it is important for us to secure our houses with maximum insulation. But given the most recent tests on available insulation, how certain can we be that the kind which we have packed into our homes is really nonflammable and is not one of the dangerously combustible brands?

Innocent household objects can be treacherous. You may remember in the late 1950s that many young children, while playing with plastic dry cleaner bags, became entangled in them and smothered. Today people often peel off the tab from the top of a cola or beer can and drop that tab into the can before they drink. An astonishing number of people have choked to death because of this practice. Yet danger may lurk not only in trivial domestic items. Even agencies designed and provided solely to protect us from death may unexpectedly destroy us. The ability of medical drugs to have harmful and even fatal side effects is probably the outstanding case. Realize the dreadful irony of such a happening: to take into ourselves a substance which is supposed to cure, but which unexpectedly (always unexpectedly!) produces harm.

If we speak of the irony of our being injured and killed by something which promises life, we must speak of one of the most baffling experiences of our time—the crisis of overpopulation. For us the production of human life, the greatest creative event which we can know, becomes an activity fraught with death. Producing life brings debility and death not by virtue of any of its side effects or its medical contingencies: it brings debility and death by its central effect of producing a human being who will have to consume food. It is destructive precisely in its life-giving power. In our day women who carry the knowledge of this grim irony must have a strange and troubled sense of themselves. They must have a very divided feeling about their fecundity. I sometimes wonder whether the movement for women's liberation at the present time may be motivated, not simply by an enthusiastic sense of women's capacities, but by this baffling fear that their life-giving power is weighted with destruction and is therefore something from which somehow they must try to separate themselves.

Now in reviewing some of these anxieties which beset people today, I do not attach significance to any of these as individual dangers. What is important is how these dangers serve to emphasize the appalling vulnerability with which we all stand before death. Of course, we can dispose of dry cleaner bags. Of course, we can establish more thorough inspections of new automobiles, household insulation, or medical drugs. But the point is not this or that hazard. The point is how subtly and insidiously death may work, how it may use as its agent the most innocent of objects and the most life-giving of activities. In one area of their consciousness Americans may devote themselves single-mindedly to life and may live out the conviction that death is removed, is outside, is somehow accidental and unnecessary. But in another area of their consciousness, they know—and they want to be reminded every day by the newspapers—that this alien can befall them at any moment. By means of the most unlikely and unforeseen of circumstances, they know and they want to be reminded constantly that they carry a vulnerability against which no amount of protection or precaution, expense or experience will help. Whatever we plan, whatever we do, we know that the mutilating power of death can attack us at any moment.

AMERICAN PESSIMISM: DEATH AS LORD

In view of this evidence, I am convinced that the bronze people (regardless of their tan skin, their confident smiles, and their scrubbed children) are haunted by the suffering, the destitution, and the death which marks the world. Despite the bronze figures which we meet in all the restaurants and advertisements, Americans seem to carry a despair about the uncanny power and pain, the uncanny destructiveness of death.

How forcibly the blues continue to dominate our popular music. What was the song of the Beatles most often played? Not an affirmative song like "She Loves You, Yah Yah Yah" or "Let It Be," but rather "Yesterday." The song presents a failure of love, a failure of life. The woman left: was she fickle, was there betrayal, or did she die? In popular songs the sense of the failure of life is overwhelming. Laughing on the outside while crying on the inside seems to be a permanent American condition. The laughing, the singing, the dancing, the assurance—these sometimes seem to be only appearances. The law of bedrock reality seems to carry the feeling of death. Therefore, a profound sense of horror breaks out and comes to clear expression in the daily press.

People themselves do not often give voice to this pessimism. One thinks of the bronze, beautiful young women by whom we are assaulted everyday in the mass media. But at another level of ourselves, we know that this beauty, this life, has no reality. John Crowe Ransom in his poem "Blue Girls" has stated this wisdom very powerfully:

Twirling your blue skirts, travelling the sward
Under the towers of your seminary,
Go listen to your teachers old and contrary
Without believing a word.

Tie the white fillets then about your hair
And think no more of what will come to pass
Than blue birds that go walking on the grass
and chattering on the air.

Practice your beauty, blue girls, before it fail;
And I will cry with my loud lips and publish
Beauty which all our power shall never establish,
It is so frail.

For I could tell you a story which is true;
I know a woman with a terrible tongue,
Blear eyes fallen from blue,
All her perfections tarnished—yet it is not long
Since she was lovelier than any of you.⁵

Here the despair perceives simply the natural, if ugly, fact of aging which mocks the freshness of youth.

Sometimes vulnerability appears as well. Perhaps one of the early dramatic instances of vulnerability was the sinking of the steamship *Titanic* in 1912. The *Titanic* had been launched with all the extremes of modern achievement in luxury and in safety. It was an expression of both resistance and success: resistance in the use of every phase of technology to anticipate disaster, and success in the feeling of security which this safety gave and in the devotion to pure life which was fostered by the opulent riches. At one level of people's awareness the fact that this modern masterpiece sank on its maiden voyage was seen simply as an accident. But there is another level of response, less clear-cut, more on the dim edge of awareness, where the sinking of the *Titanic* marked total vulnerability. It took the forces of nature to find and exploit that vulnerability.

Thomas Hardy gives voice to this pessimistic awareness in "The Convergence of the Twain." He begins by describing the ship, resting at the bottom of the ocean.

I

In a solitude of the sea
Deep from human vanity,
And the Pride of Life that planned here, stilly couches she.

II

Steel chambers, late the pyres
Of her salamandrine fire,
Cold currents thrid, and thurn to rhythmic tidal lyres.

III

Over the mirrors meant
To glass the opulent
The sea-worm crawls—grotesque, slimed, dumb, indifferent.

IV

Jewels in joy designed
To ravish the sensuous mind
Lie lightless, all their sparkles bleared and black and blind.

V

Dim moon-eyed fishes near
Gaze at the gilded gear
And query: 'What does this vaingloriousness down here?' . . .

VI

Well: while was fashioning
This creature of cleaving wing,
The Immanent Will that stirs and urges everything

VII

Prepared a sinister mate
For her—so gaily great—
A Shape of Ice, for the time far and dissociate.

VIII

And as the smart ship grew
In stature, grace, and hue,
In shadowy silent distance grew the Iceberg too.

IX

Alien they seemed to be:
No mortal eye could see
The intimate welding of their later history,

X

Or sign that they were bent
By paths coincident
On being anon twin halves of one august event,

XI

Till the Spinner of the Years
Said 'Now!' And each one hears,
And consummation comes, and jars two hemispheres.[6]

Hardy catches the dreadful sense of something uncanny and malevolent in the way seemingly fortuitous events can join to bring disaster. Why did that poor person have to be driving on that part of the highway just at that moment when the drunken driver appeared? Both poems, Ransom's and Hardy's, focus on a single detail.

Sometimes this pessimism can envelop the whole world. All of us have moments in our daily routine when a kind of immense pervasive pessimism can momentarily grip us. It is precisely this momentary experience which James Joyce presents in his novel *Ulysses*. Leopold Bloom is walking toward a restaurant for lunch.

> His smile faded as he walked, a heavy cloud hiding the sun slowly, shadowing Trinity's surly front. Trams passed one another, ingoing, outgoing, clanging. Useless words. Things go on same; day after day: squads of police marching out, back: trams in, out. Those two loonies mooching about. Dignam carted off. Mina Purefoy swollen belly on a bed groaning to have a child tugged out of her. One born every second somewhere. Other dying every second. Since I fed the birds five minutes. Three hundred kicked the bucket. Other three hundred born, washing the blood off, all are washed in the blood of the lamb, bawling maaaaaa.

Then suddenly Bloom's sense of this routine, this empty routine, expands into the whole vision of human history.

> Cityful passing away, other cityful coming, passing away too: other coming on, passing on. Houses, lines of houses, streets, miles of pavements, piledup bricks, stones. Changing hands. This owner, that. Landlord never dies they say. Other steps into his shoes when he gets his notice to quit.

Then he has the vision of the end of the city.

> They buy the place up with gold and still they have all the gold. Swindle in it somewhere. Piled up in cities, worn away age after age. Pyramids in sand. Built on bread and onions. Slaves. Chinese wall. Babylon. Big stones left. Round towers.

Then he considers the end of the modern city.

> Rest rubble, sprawling suburbs, jerrybuilt, Kerwan's mushroom houses, built of breeze. Shelter for the night.

No one is anything.

This is the very worst hour of the day. Vitality. Dull, gloomy: hate this hour. Feel as if I had been eaten and spewed.[7]

In this passage the city becomes the figure for the collective life and effort of human beings. What is the outcome of even the greatest cities? Rubbish. But the modern spreads of jerry-built houses will not leave even a trace. Here the sense of the power of death and the utter vulnerability of life yields a vision of a totally meaningless world.

So the last and final question must be asked. It is always being asked in each of us. Is life really worth living? Does good come? Will a future bear more promise than the present? Or are all human values and aspirations just a deceit by which people motivate themselves in a pointless world that goes nowhere but toward death? The ancient Greeks had a story about Silenus that poses this last and final question very grimly. According to the story King Midas searched in the woods a long time for Silenus, the companion of Dionysius. At last Silenus fell into his hands. When the king asked him what was the best and most desirable of all things for human persons, the demigod said nothing for some time. At last under the king's urgings he gave a shrill laugh and said, "Oh wretched, passing race, children of chance and misery, why do you force me to tell you what it were better for you not to hear. What is best is beyond your reach forever. That is not to be born, not to be, to be nothing at all. And the second best for you is to die quickly."[8]

Now what are we to make of this pessimism, this sense of the power of death and human helplessness? What are we to make of the daily papers? Let us not ask yet whether this is a true account of the world. For the moment let us suspend that question. Let us ask what does this pessimism say about the character of the American people? It seems to me this despair signifies immediately the extreme American sensitivity to suffering and death. It shows Americans to be a very civilized and refined people. Torture, brutality, pain, and human destruction are intolerable for them, almost unendurable. I read their sense of the great power of death and its mutilation, not primarily as an effort by Americans to give an objective account of what the world is really like. Rather it indicates what they find really dreadful, what acts powerfully upon their sensitivity, what offends and lacerates them. We do not understand it. We protest against it. But our protest is useless, even worse than useless. Even the drugs we use to fight it can become its instruments for our destruction.

AN ARTISTIC TRIUMPH

We can now understand the ethics of avoidance and resistance as our protest which arises out of a refined and civilized intolerance toward death. Here we can locate all the optimistic confidence in life, all the passion for success among the bronze people, and all the passion for service among those who help the unfortunate. This whole realm of successful life (even for the people who live by it) is only a dream, only an illusion, only an imaginative creation like a work of art. It is not ever thought to be real, to pertain to the bedrock nature of actual human existence. The optimism is contrived appearance; the success is a contrived appearance; the gratitude to God and helping the unfortunate are only contrived appearances. Americans know, at some deep level, that every generation will suffer like its predecessors and will die like them. Foam rubber mattresses, anesthetics, fast airplanes, and color TVs—these do not enhance the quality of inner life. These do not make human life any less a plaything for death. But these do help to create an illusory realm of success and happiness: a realm without pain, without failure, without destitution and death; an illusory realm so centered in life that on Sunday afternoons in the fall, the spectacle of twenty-two adult men running around after a bag of air is enough to provide millions of people with zest and joy.

The optimism is known to be an illusion. But, like a work of art, it is serious and important because it is a work of the imagination. This illusory world is critical, in fact, because it performs an absolutely important function for the American people. It helps them conceal the horror of life which they half know to be there. In order for these sensitive Americans psychically to endure their existence at all, they have to interpose between themselves and actual life a dream world of success and cleanliness and health and beauty and perpetual youth. All the terribleness of existence reflected in our newspapers, the savagery of death, the extent of mass starvation, the sly forms of injury and hurt—all this is overcome, not in the fabric of real human existence, but with the aid of a fabricated world of happy and secure aliveness. Or to put it better, all this horror is veiled and concealed by the world of nice appearances. If Americans were not able to lose themselves in a contrived and tranquil realm of fabricated security, how could Americans endure real existence for one moment?

But notice what happens once they create this idealized world of vigor, health, and well-being in an unbroken network of appearances. Then life within this illusory realm becomes a good in itself, a good that justifies itself. Here all the monsters are slain, all the demons removed, all the nightmares abolished. Here, in the words of the advertisement, "Pain is removed, disease is cured, injustice is abolished, and hunger is ended." Here the wisdom of Silenus is reversed. People commit themselves to this realm of nice appearances and do not fear death, do not long for death. No, just the opposite: they long for life, life, and more life. Death has become an unnecessary accident. Now, the worst of all is to die young, and second worst is to die at all. The artistic and fabricating impulse has triumphed over that terrible awareness that Americans have of dreadful reality and over their intense sensitivity to suffering. So Americans let themselves become fully absorbed in the appearances of life, in the clean air, in the nice lawn, in the streets without beggars, in the homes without the aged. In truth reality is intolerable. Fabricating this illusory world is a high and necessary calling. *The bronze people should not be denigrated.* They exist to veil the horror, and their obligation, therefore, is to be as purely bronzed as possible. They must exclude every appearance of pain and death, even if inside they know pain and feel the approach of death.

In the United States the primary instrument for creating this illusory world is technology. Technology is not used to effect reality; it is used to create and maintain this world of illusory life. And it is illusion. People brag about the changes that go on today, but these are changes only on the surface. Television, airplanes, medicine, industry—these do not change the essential fabric of life, even though they do give speed, efficiency, and vigor to the realm of appearance. Black Americans have not been restored to dignity. But on the level of appearances in the mass media great advances have been made. And what does it mean to advance black people? What are we going to do, take away their hunger and give them middle-class neuroses instead?

We must note clearly that this optimistic world of illusion is rooted in the world where suffering and death reign uncontrolled. The more clearly Americans perceive grim horror and senseless suffering in their actual existence and the more eagerly they long for release, the more they are compelled to believe that this realm of happy, healthy appearances is real. The more they wrap themselves in those appearances, in the comfortable and peaceful suburban streets, the more they will say that the dreadful things are merely appearances. "I'm not really getting old (it only looks that way)." "I'm not cut off from love (my divorce only makes it look that way)." "I'm not essentially sick in my being (I simply have some symptoms, that is, some appearances which my doctor will remove)." Now the dreadful things are accidents and mistakes. They do not belong and they will disappear.

The whole American venture into health and success and beauty and vigor, the whole existence which Americans try to live with all their consciousness rests on the hidden substratum of suffering and dreadful knowledge. The bronze world of youthful beauty and the mutilated figures spilled over the highway are interdependent. They belong together. You remember how *Life* magazine would have a picture of some lovely young woman advertising soap on the left side and then, on the right side, would present a picture of unmitigated brutality? Yet it never occurred to the editors or most readers to see any incongruity. In the United States these two visions of life belong together. The old minstrel song is pertinent: "Because my mouth is wide with laughter and my throat is deep with song, you do not think I suffer after I've held my pain so long. Because my mouth is wide with laughter, you do not hear my inner cry. Because my feet are gay with dancing, you do not know I die?" I am convinced that the American joy of life, its style of success, and its passion for service are all born out of the heart of darkness and are established on the anguishing knowledge of pain.

THE DIMLY KNOWN

What should we say of the ethic of success in the bronze dream? Do Americans believe in such optimism? The answer, I think, is both yes and no. They do believe in this optimism as the rule for their own existence. Refusing to be lacerated by the horrors of life, they create their world of life-affirming buoyancy. They teach their children to be self-confident. They sequester their failures in institutions out of sight. But Americans know that the whole bronze dream is no more than appearance. It is that and it is important as that. The dream veils from them the nightmares, but it does not affect reality. We color the greying hair, but nothing is really affected. We keep the house neat and clean, but the marriage continues to strain. We sequester our unfortunates but they still suffer, hidden from our notice. The degree to which people see real human existence as the helpless plaything of death is the degree to which they are content with the triumph of life at the level of appearances, with the removal of death at the level of appearances.

What do people see as the bedrock actual? I think that at a deep, silent, and despairing level within themselves many Americans see the sort of thing that Kenneth Fearing describes in his poem "American Rhapsody II."

First you bite your fingernails. And then you comb your hair again. And then you wait. And wait.
(They say, you know, that first you lie. And then you steal, they say. And then, they say, you kill.)

Then the doorbell rings. Then Peg drops in. And Bill. And Jane. And Doc.
And first you talk, and smoke, and hear the news and have a drink.
   And you dine, then, and go to a show after that, perhaps, and after that a night spot, and after that come home again, and climb the stairs again, and again go to bed.

But first Peg argues, and Doc replies. First you dance the same dance and you drink the same drink you always drank before.
And the piano builds a roof of notes above the world.
And the trumpet weaves a dome of music through space. And the drum makes a ceiling over space and time and night.
And then the table-wit. And then the check. Then home again to bed.
But first, the stairs.

And do you now, baby, as you climb the stairs, do you still feel as you felt back there?
Do you feel again as you felt this morning? And the night before?
   And then the night before that?

(They say, you know, that first you hear voices. And then you have visions, they say. Then, they say, you kick and scream and rave.)
Or do you feel: What is one more night in a lifetime of nights?
What is one more death, or friendship, or divorce out of two, or three? Or four? Or five?
One more face among so many, many faces, one more life among so many million lives?

But first, baby, as you climb and count the stairs (and they total the same) did you, sometime or somewhere, have a different idea?
Is this, baby, what you were born to feel, and do, and be?[9]

Is this what we were born to feel and do and be? Not at all. And so, many American people work to create and maintain the beautiful world of bronze appearances where people never look as if they were going to die.

If we ask about religion in America, you can see the conclusion which I must draw. The God whom Americans worship as the final and absolute Lord of reality is the power of death. Here I do not use the term "god" to designate the divinity revealed in Jesus Christ. I use the word in a more open way, to name what a people believe to be the final, the ultimate reality which controls their lives. Many Americans (notwithstanding their dedicated commitment to the ethics of success and of resistance) still believe that death is the ultimate reality which will finally and permanently determine their existence. Thomas Hardy's sense of that fateful spinner of the years, Leopold Bloom's sense of the movement of history toward rubbish, Kenneth Fearing's sense of the person in the modern city, abandoned and meaningless—for many of us, these are the images of the ultimate with which we must finally *reckon.*

I am convinced that even many American Christians share this belief in the divinity of death. But what of the Christian God, the God of love and kindness? Ah, you see, God rules the realm of appearances. This one is the God of the illusory world. It is the Christian God who helps veil the horror. Do American Christians honestly believe that love rules this present world, rules the city, rules the home, rules the international scene? Not really. But in the realm of fabricated appearances, there love can rule and there the God of love can have a kingdom. And as the crucial figure in the illusory world, the Christian God helps us veil and endure this nightmare world.

There is a scene in the novel *Catch 22* by Joseph Heller which bears on this situation. Yossarian, the main character, is an Air Corps Officer in Italy during the Second World War. In this scene, he is in the hospital, carrying his normal temperature of 102. Lieutenant Scheisskopf's wife is visiting him; it is Thanksgiving Day.

> It was the most rational Thanksgiving he had ever spent, and he took a sacred oath to spend every future Thanksgiving Day in the cloistered shelter of a hospital. He broke his sacred oath the very next year when he spent the holiday in a hotel room instead in intellectual conversation with Lieutenant Scheisskopf's wife, who had Dori Duz's dog tags on for the occasion and who henpecked Yossarian sententiously for being cynical and callous about Thanksgiving, even though she didn't believe in God just as much as he didn't.
>
> "I'm probably just as good an atheist as you are," she speculated boastfully. "But even I feel that we all have a great deal to be thankful for and that we shouldn't be ashamed to show it."

"Name one thing I've got to be thankful for," Yossarian challenged her without interest.

"Well . . ." Lieutenant Scheisskopf's wife mused and paused a moment to ponder dubiously. "Me."

"Oh, come on," he scoffed.

She arched her eyebrows in surprise. "Aren't you thankful for me?" she asked. She frowned peevishly, her pride wounded. "I don't have to shack up with you, you know. . . ."

So she continues.

"Be thankful you've got me," she insisted.

"I am, honey. But I'm also goddam good and miserable that I can't have Dori Duz again, too. Or the hundreds of other girls and women I'll see and want in my short lifetime and won't be able to go to bed with even once."

"Be thankful you're healthy."

"Be bitter you're not going to stay that way."

"Be glad you're even alive."

"Be *furious* you're going to die."

"Things could be much worse," she cried.

"They could be one hell of a lot better," he answered heatedly. . . .

"And don't tell me God works in mysterious ways," Yossarian continued. . . . "There's nothing so mysterious about it. He's not working at all. He's playing. Or else He's forgotten all about us. That's the kind of God you people talk about—a country bumpkin, a clumsy, bungling, brainless, conceited, uncouth hayseed. Good God, how much reverence can you have for a Supreme Being who finds it necessary to include such phenomena as phlegm and tooth decay in His divine system of creation? What in the world was running through that warped, evil, scatological mind of His when He robbed old people of the power to control their bowel movements? Why in the world did He ever create pain?"

"Pain?" Lieutenant Scheisskopf's wife pounced upon the word victoriously. "Pain is a useful symptom. Pain is a warning to us of bodily dangers."

"And who created the dangers?" Yossarian demanded. He laughed caustically. "Oh, He was really being charitable to us when He gave us pain! Why couldn't He have used a doorbell instead to notify us, or one of His celestial choirs? . . . What a colossal, immortal blunderer! When you consider the opportunity and power He had to really do a job, and then look at the stupid, ugly little mess He made of it instead, His sheer incompetence is almost staggering. It's obvious He never met a payroll. Why, no self-respecting businessman would hire a bungler like Him as even a shipping clerk!"

Lieutenant Scheisskopf's wife had turned ashen in disbelief and was ogling him with alarm. "You'd better not talk that way about Him, honey," she warned him reprovingly . . . "He might punish you."

"Isn't He punishing me enough?" Yossarian snorted resentfully. "You know, we mustn't let Him get away with it. Oh, no, we certainly mustn't let

Him get away scot free for all the sorrow He's caused us. Someday I'm going to make Him pay. I know when. On the Judgment Day. Yes, that's the day I'll be close enough to reach out and grab that little yokel by His neck and—"

"Stop it! Stop it!" Lieutenant Scheisskopf's wife screamed suddenly, and began beating him infectually about the head with both fists. "Stop it!"

Yossarian ducked behind his arm for protection while she slammed away at him in feminine fury for a few seconds. . . . "What the hell are you getting so upset about?" he asked her bewilderedly in a tone of contrite amusement. "I thought you didn't believe in God."

"I don't," she sobbed, bursting violently into tears. "But the God I don't believe in is a good God, a just God, a merciful God. He's not the mean and stupid God you make Him out to be."[10]

The Yossarian which Heller presents here represents the person who rejects the illusory world, who looks upon the horror and is appalled. All he can do is make a pointless gesture of wanting to judge this torturing, evil god and make him pay for the unmitigated agony which his creation produces. Yossarian expresses, I suppose, that sense of pointless human suffering which has been the main source of atheism in the twentieth century. But Yossarian's attitude is not common in our country. I find Lt. Scheisskopf's wife more representative of Americans. The world is awful, but Americans usually do not say so. Instead they have a good and loving god. This god is not real. Death is real. But like tan skin and regular exercise and peaceful neighborhoods, this god belongs to the realm of illusion, by which Americans are able to shield themselves from the awfulness of life, from the torment and destitution which always threaten to overwhelm their sensitivity.

This concludes my account of a complex and two-sided strand in the American attitude toward death. The burden of the next three chapters can be put quite simply. In the light of Jesus Christ death becomes a venture within our moral possibility. It becomes something we may freely choose. In other words, in the light of Jesus Christ death ceases to be some enormity from which we have to be saved. It is desacralized. It loses all its ultimacy. In the remaining chapters I will look at three distinct ways in which death is diminished by Jesus Christ to our human measure.

NOTES

1. *Washington Post*, 14 July 1974.
2. Albert Camus, *The Plague*, trans. Stewart Gilbert (New York: The Modern Library, 1948), 34–35.

3. See Rheingold, *The Mother, Anxiety and Death*, chap. 1.

4. See McGill, *Suffering*, chap. 2. See also William F. May, "The Sacral Power of Death in Contemporary Experience," *Social Research* 39 (Fall 1972): 463–88; and idem, "The Metaphysical Plight of the Family," in *Death Inside Out*, 49–60. May, like McGill, offers an account of death as a religious experience. Both build upon the work of Gerardus van der Leeuw, *Religion in Essence and Manifestation*, trans. J. E. Turner (London: George Allen & Unwin, 1938).

5. John Crowe Ransom, "Blue Girls," in *Selected Poems*, 3d ed. (New York: Alfred A. Knopf, 1969), 11.

6. Thomas Hardy, "The Convergence of the Twain," in *The Complete Poems of Thomas Hardy*, ed. James Gibson (New York: Macmillan, 1978), 306–7.

7. James Joyce, *Ulysses* (New York: The Modern Library, 1961), 164.

8. Friedrich Nietzsche, *The Birth of Tragedy*, in *Basic Writings of Nietzsche*, trans. and ed. Walter Kaufman (New York: The Modern Library, 1968), 42–43.

9. Kenneth Fearing, "American Rhapsody II," in *New and Selected Poems* (Bloomington: Indiana Univ. Press, 1956), 79–80.

10. Joseph Heller, *Catch 22* (New York: Simon and Schuster, 1961).

3

In Christ the Transformation of the Self Involves—Death

THEOLOGICAL METHOD

I will now describe my method in this book. I am convinced that we human beings do not relate to life and death in terms of ideas and concepts, or in terms of abstract generalities. Life is concrete. Death is concrete. We know life and death in and with our bodies. I think, therefore, that we secure our sense of life and our sense of death from images. These images are not creatures of fancy. They are incidents or situations which we encounter in our real existence. But they are incidents or situations in which the truth about life and death seems to be disclosed to us. Therefore, whenever I reflect about life and death, I must always focus on key images. If I ask about how a people feel about life and death, I look for images by which they express their awareness of these mysteries. And if I believe someone's sense of life and death is wrong, I do so because I reject the images that shape that person's sense and find my guidance from other images.

The previous two chapters have really been an elaboration of two images which control a prevailing sense of life and death in the United States. I gave an account of life excluding death, as having no essential relation to death and as entailing the ethic of success where all negatives are avoided and the ethic of resistance and service where victims of suffering are given help. This whole sketch was really only an elaboration of that image of life provided by the bronze people. It is not this idea of life as free from death which is primary in the American experience, nor its ethic of success and service. What is primary is *seeing* bronze people—on the beach, in the restaurants, in the advertisements—and believing that there, in them, we have actualized what life really is. The second chapter gave an account of the deep sense of death as violent power, as a kind of active energy that mutilates and seems able to attack us at any moment. This too was only an elaboration of those images of the dreadful automobile accidents which come to us in the daily press.

These two images I find absolutely central and controlling in the American sense of life and death. But they stand in contrast to each other. First, there may be a lovely young blonde woman in a swimsuit telling me to drink orange juice in order to be as healthy and happy as she seems, in a universe where every hint of death has been removed. Alongside is another picture, also of a young blonde woman (and for all I know, it may be the same woman who has been telling me about orange juice) who has been crushed to death in an automobile. In order to understand how these two contradictory images are related, I have suggested that the destructive and demonic power of death is really believed to be the Lord of actual reality, as God for most Americans. Remember I do not use the word "god" to designate the divinity revealed in Jesus Christ. I use it in a more open way to name whatever someone believes to be the final, the ultimate reality which controls his or her life.

Most Americans (and that includes many who go regularly to church) believe that death is the ultimate reality which will finally and permanently determine their existence. The power of death, then, is the true God. That is to say, the auto accident reveals to many Americans the power that, at the last horizon, rules this world absolutely. On that basis the character of our defense and the character of our life make very good sense. What of the bronze life then? I made the suggestion that it is known only as a realm of appearance. It is a dream world of illusion. But for a people as sensitive to suffering and death as we Americans, this illusory world helps to veil the real horror, the real savagery and brutality of existence. Given a universe where death is final and absolute and against which the human race has no effective power at all, then the highest human thing is to say "No" to that brutality. We must say no, even if that no makes no final difference, even if it can only be the creation of a make-believe world of clean and happy appearances. The appearances change nothing; the power of mutilating death still rules all things without exception. No amount of bronze healthiness keeps cancer away. Yet by committing ourselves imaginatively and fictively in a make-believe illusion, we humans do say no to the dreadfulness of death. We do put a veil of pleasing appearances over the unbearable horrors which actually surround us.

For many Americans the Christian God of love is not the real God at all. This god is only part of the illusory world of appearances. People would like this god to be real—my goodness yes! People try to live their make-believe lives as if this god were real. Yet on another level of their minds they believe that, for themselves, for all their values, and for all their loved ones, the final and ultimate god will be, not the Father of Jesus Christ, but the mutilating power of death.

We turn now from the American attitudes to ask this question: what is the meaning of life and death for the Christian tradition? In order to answer this question, I will not go to theologians with their conceptual and abstract ideas. Nor will I go to ethicists with their accounts of values and duties. I will ask instead: What are the absolutely decisive images through which the Christian sense of life and death has been shaped? The answer is obvious. The decisive images are of Jesus Christ, especially as presented in the New Testament. So far as theologians have ideas about life and death and so far as ethicists discern commands about life and death, they simply elaborate what is imaged forth in the presentation of Jesus from the New Testament. In the remaining chapters I will sketch what is imaged about life and death by the Jesus given in the New Testament.

A WILL TOWARD DEATH

Both of the images which dominate the American scene today have a place within the horizon of Jesus. On the one hand, the New Testament accounts of the resurrected life, the life that belongs in perfect harmony with God, speak in exactly the same way as the bronze dream. Death has no place in that life. In fact, we might say that the American idea of the successful life (in which death has no essential place) is a secularized version of the New Testament sense of the resurrected life. On the other hand, Jesus' crucifixion represents as powerful an image of the demonic and mutilating power of death as any auto accident or hydrogen bomb. That the Son of God should be hung on a cross and executed in this most

gruesome way certainly pictures the awesome power of death. Neverthe-
less, the image of Jesus is basically different from either of these American
images. The resurrected life and the crucifixion both represent moments
in the New Testament's presentation of Jesus. But neither is the center.
Jesus is not presented primarily as a victim of death like the people who are
shown killed in automobiles. Nor is Jesus presented primarily as enjoying
the life free from all death which the bronze people seek.

In one decisive way Jesus stands in complete contrast to the images
provided by the bronze people and by the mutilated corpse. Jesus *chooses to
die.* His life is not taken from him against his will. Jesus lays down his life of
his own will. The four gospel narratives, in fact, present Jesus' whole mis-
sion and meaning as directed to his dying. He comes to die. His death is
not a kind of unfortunate accident, a regrettable mishap, which might not
have happened if Jesus had been fortunate to live in a free society where
individual rights are protected and honored. He is not a bronze person
with death completely outside of and unrelated to the center and essence
of his existence. In fact, he is just the opposite of a bronze person. He
comes with dying the focus and center of his existence. Therefore, in the
Gospel of Luke when the infant Jesus is taken to the temple to be circum-
sized, the aged priest Simon declares to Mary the meaning of Jesus' existence: "This child is destined to be a sign which [humans] reject; and you
too shall be pierced to the heart" (Luke 2:34–35, NEB).

Jesus' death, moreover, is not a fateful fatality like the image of the
automobile accident. It does not serve to show how humans, in spite of all
their passion for life, can be wiped out in a moment's notice. By his death
Jesus does not represent the enormity of the power of death. On the contrary, he chooses to die. He lays down his life freely and deliberately, and
he does so in accord with God's own will. Jesus' death is just the opposite
of an unexpected, unforeseen auto accident. For the New Testament there
is absolutely nothing accidental at all about Jesus' death. It belongs to his
conscious purpose; it is grounded in God's loving will. Far from proclaim-
ing the mutilating power of death (as does a nuclear bomb), Jesus' death
takes death out of the demonic and makes it an event informed by the free
decision of this man and by the graciousness of this God.

Precisely because they see death as the complete negation of life, many
Americans remain Christians only by denying that Jesus wants to die and
that he means to die. Similarly, they must deny that it is God's will that
they too should deliberately live toward death. From the viewpoint that

now prevails in the United States, the way of Jesus is suicide, and no Christian advocates that people lay down their lives. On this view, the Christian way opposes death, fights death, helps all sick and deprived people, keeps away from death as long as possible—that is the will of God as worshiped by the bronze people. Many American Christians (and perhaps many American Christian ministers also) will not hear of the Jesus who deliberately lays down his life on God's initiative and expects all his followers to do the same.

As I reflect on Jesus I will focus especially on one aspect of the kind of life and death which he images: on the fact that he wills to die and that he calls his followers also to die. Why? What is being shown about life and death in the way in which Jesus wills this death and wills it for us? In this chapter I will consider the reason which Paul gives in Romans 6. Paul has just spoken of the fact that sin has served to show forth the graciousness of God. He writes:

> What are we to say, then? Shall we persist in sin, so that there may be all the more grace? No, no! We died to sin: how can we live in it any longer? Have you forgotten that when we were baptized into union with Christ Jesus we were baptized into his death? By baptism we were buried with him, and we lay dead, in order that, as Christ was raised from the dead in the splendor of the Father, so also we might set our feet upon the new path of life. For if we have become incorporate with him in a death like his, we shall also be one with him in a resurrection like his. We know that the [person] we once were has been crucified with Christ, for the destruction of the sinful self, so that we may no longer be slaves of sin, since a dead [person] is no longer answerable for sin. But if we thus died with Christ, we believe that we shall also come to life with him. We know that Christ, once raised from the dead, is never to die again; he is no longer under the dominion of death. For in dying as he died, he died to sin, once and for all, and in living as he lives, he lives to God. In the same way you must regard yourselves as dead to sin and alive to God, in union with Christ Jesus. So sin must no longer reign in your mortal body (Rom. 6:1–12a, NEB).

Here we have one familiar interpretation of Jesus' laying down his life. Jesus dies to destroy the power of sin in human existence, so that by Jesus' resurrection in the splendor of God the Father we too may live with him in that newness of life. In dying as Jesus dies (not as we ordinarily die, but as he died), he dies to sin once for all. And living as he lives, he lives to God. So we too, in union with Jesus Christ, must regard ourselves as dead to sin and alive to God.

Paul's passage, however, is much easier to read than to understand. In order to understand it we will have to consider the two topics which it presents. First, it sets a contrast between one kind of human existence which *is enslaved to sin and ruled by death* and another kind of human existence which *lives to God, free from the power of death*. What is this sin? What is this life which lives to God? Second, the passage asserts that the way we humans may move from one condition to the other is by dying with Jesus Christ. The person we are must be crucified with Christ for the destruction of that sinful self so that we may no longer be slaves of sin. But as we thus die with Christ, we believe that we shall also come to life with him. What does it mean to die with Christ? And how does it come about? These two topics and their accompanying questions need to be considered in detail.

There is a strong tradition which views sin as moral, as misdirected will. This view comes primarily from the influence of the Old Testament. The Lord God said to Israel: "This day I set before you the way of life and the way of death. Choose" (Deut. 30:19, NEB). Sin is often taken then to be a wrong choice, a choice not in accord with God's will. Here sin belongs properly and essentially to our acts of will. It characterizes any wanting that we do which is against what God commands. This is not Paul's view. In fact, such an understanding of sin makes nonsense of the passage in Romans 6. If sin is a matter of making a wrong choice, then the overcoming of sin involves us in making a right choice. It involves us in acts of our will—exactly what Paul denies we can do. Paul did not write that through union with Jesus' death we are prompted to give up making sinful choices and begin making righteous choices; thus our sinful self is destroyed and we are no longer slaves to sin. Paul would have nothing to do with the idea that sin is a matter of our willing. Instead, Paul insists that through union with Jesus' death, *we die*. We are buried with him and we lay dead. Thus our sinful self is destroyed, and we are no longer slaves of sin. If sin were simply a matter of wrong choices, it would not require us to die and to lie dead in order to be free from sin. It would only require us to change our decisions.

The moral tradition of the United States, therefore, has been quite unable to deal with this text. In a basic sense, dying means that our identity is destroyed. If we can be free from sin only by dying, then sin must be a matter, not of our willing, but of our basic identity. I do not need death to change my decisions or to change my ideas or to change my attitudes;

but *I do need death to change my basic and fundamental identity*, to change the way in which I am real and the way in which I try to be real. Paul believes that through Jesus we may all have a new morality, a set of new mental attitudes. But these new attitudes are the consequence of having a new sense of our identity, a new sense of how we are real.

For instance in Romans Paul does not simply say, "Let your minds be remade." He says, "Let your minds be remade and your whole nature be thus transformed" (Rom. 12:2, NEB). In Eph. 4:22–24 the author does not write, "Leave your former way of life." He writes, "Leaving your former way of life, you must lay aside that old human nature which . . . is sinking towards death. You must be made new in mind and spirit, and put on the new nature of God's creating, which shows itself in the just and devout life" (NEB). That is to say, for the new Christian morality the just and devout life is simply the way in which the new nature, or what I am calling the *new identity*, shows itself. And of course, to get a new identity we have to lose our old identity. That loss is exactly the nature of death.

What are these two contrary identities? What are these two natures, one of which Paul calls "sin" and the other he calls "living-to-God"? How are these two ways of being so totally different that one can be present only through the removal or death of the other? Paul characterizes the resurrected life as a matter of our belonging to God: "For though everything belongs to you . . . yet you belong to Christ, and Christ to God" (1 Cor. 3:22–23, NEB). Paul also thinks of the resurrected life as a matter of our acknowledging that all our power comes from God, or as a matter of honoring God as God, and being thankful to God always for everything. Let me try to interpret Paul's view of this new kind of identity, this new way of being, by noting something *peculiar* about Jesus.

THE ECSTATIC IDENTITY OF JESUS

In the New Testament portrayal of Jesus, nothing is more striking than the lack of interest in Jesus' own personality. His teachings and miracles, the response of the crowd and the hostility of the authorities, his dying and his resurrection—these are not read as windows into Jesus' own experience, feelings, insights, and growth. In other words, the *center* of Jesus' reality is not within Jesus himself. Everything that happens to him, everything that is done by him, including his death, is displaced to another context and is thereby reinterpreted. However, this portrayal is understood to be a true reflection of Jesus' own way of existing. He himself does not live out of himself. He lives, so to speak, from beyond himself. Jesus does not confront his followers as a center which reveals himself. He confronts them as always revealing what is beyond him. In that sense Jesus lives what I call an *ecstatic identity*.

In all the early testimony to Jesus, this peculiar characteristic is identified with the fact that Jesus knows that his reality comes from God. Basic to his self-consciousness is his constant awareness of God as his Father, of God as his ongoing basis and origin. In Jesus' apprehension of God as his origin, God does not function as an external cause that once created him in the past, but rather as a presently and continually operative cause, as a causing. Such a sense of origin entails a complete reordering of the usual understanding of a person's relation to God. God does not create a person by conferring some reality unto that person. God does not create by so securing a person with being that he or she exists by virtue of a reality which God has imparted. If that were the case, people would know and be themselves simply by taking possession of their own reality, simply by being one with themselves. Then there would be a second and subsequent act in which a person would recognize that this being, which he or she is from God, came from God.

Jesus' oddity lies in the fact that there is no moment when, to himself or before others, he is simply the reality which he possesses, no moment when he is simply his own self, so that he has to execute a special shift of attention in order to become aware of God. Rather, in the act of knowing himself, he also knows God, immediately. He knows the constituting activity of God as the constant and ongoing condition of his own being. Jesus never has his own being; he is continually receiving it. No reality at all is ever conferred over to him as his own and made the content of some secure identity. He is only as one who keeps receiving himself from God. He is always a son. Herein lies the ecstatic character of Jesus' identity.

In the case of Jesus, and those who are remade in his image, this ecstatic identity means that the normal simple sense of "I am" is altered. Normally, identity is determined by drawing a boundary. Everything outside the boundary is not me, while all the content within the boundary is taken as constituting me—my property, my books, my children, my body, my memory. In other words, this simple kind of identity takes its model from material objects, specifically from the human body. Jesus' kind of ecstatic identity shatters this simple, this direct "I am." "I am" now becomes complex. I am no longer that part of reality which has been delivered over to me, which now belongs stably to me. Rather, I am by virtue of a constant receiving. My "I am" exists by virtue of an activity that constantly comes from beyond myself. Relative to the normal sense of identity, such a development can only appear as a self-alienation, a self-disruption. The center within me is no longer the core of my reality. My being constantly comes from beyond me. Hence, I am no longer just myself, just the being which I already have, just the being which is at my disposal. My "I am" necessarily and constantly includes God's activity of constituting me.

THE NEW IDENTITY

When Paul speaks in Romans 6 of becoming incorporate with Jesus Christ so that we die to sin and live to God, I understand this living-to-God as living always related to God, living always open to God, in the act of receiving oneself from God. Living an ecstatic identity, then, is the new kind of identity, the new way of being, which we secure through Jesus Christ. It is a new kind of human nature which shows itself in a just and devout life, which gives us a new mind and a new morality. When we have this sense of ourselves as what we constantly receive from God's free giving, what do we experience when we experience ourselves? *We experience love.* We experience this love not primarily in terms of receiving the goods of this world or in terms of being protected from the evils of this world. We experience this love primarily in terms of receiving ourselves and being ourselves. And when we experience ourselves as a gift, as a free, joyful, and continual gift, we are filled with that feeling which Paul placed first of all in the new life—*the feeling of gratitude.*

Gratitude does not arise because, while being myself, it now and then occurs to me to remember that this self which I now possess once upon a time came originally from God. To feel gratitude I do not have to be reminded of God as if God were somewhere away outside of me. God is related to me constantly in every instant of my being. In being myself (which means in receiving myself from God's love) I feel gratitude as a basic and continuing feeling. More than that, because I no longer live by virtue of the reality which I possess, which I hold, which I master and keep at my disposal, I am free to share myself and all my possessions with others. Above all and most important for Paul, I can be honest with others. I can let myself be open before them. I do not have to draw a line to mark the boundaries of my reality where I place a sign which says "Keep Out." I do not have to conceal my being behind a wall in order to keep it mine and to prevent others from taking it from me. Since I never have myself, I can never be dispossessed of myself. In short, in all my relations with other people I am freed from the anxiety of having always to keep possession of my own reality in order to be.

If we look upon the character and goal of human life from this vantage point, we can see one of the saddest features of existence for most people. They keep running out into the world looking for love, looking for someone to love them and cherish them, for someone to honor and dignify them. They do not realize that just in being themselves they are experiencing the love of God at the very center of their being. In order to find love, none of us needs to go out looking in the world for some supportive community or for some cherishing person. The love that passes understanding is available to us in the very act of our being, because we are constantly receiving that from our God.

If love is simply being ourselves, then we need to reconsider the doctrine of creation. As it is usually presented, the doctrine of creation tries to tell us that God created the world, that the world is the product of God's love; therefore, if we are to know the goodness of God's love, we must go out into the world. But such a presentation is a dangerous and perverse set of ideas. Such ideas take us away from the place where God's love is most intimately known: not out in the world, but in receiving ourselves continually from God.

WAGES OF SIN

There is another element in Paul's contrast. What does he mean by sin? Or better, what does Paul mean by an identity-in-sin? Identity-in-sin means not to live from God, not to honor God as the constant source of our being, not to be thankful to God as the one who constantly gives us ourselves. *Identity is sin* when persons imagine that their being has been conferred over to them, when they try to live out of themselves in terms of the reality which God may have once conferred onto them but which they now hold in their own possession. Sin is to refuse to live out of the reality which a person constantly receives from God. It is the pride, the self-glory, which Paul sees as sinful identity.

If we think of sin as this way of being, as an identity by self-possession, then we can see that sinful self-identity has to live by a specific set of principles. For instance, what is good and desirable and valuable for me when I live this kind of identity? It is good for me to secure reality into my control and possession, and the more reality the better. I can do this securing two possible ways. First, I may try to seize bits of the world for myself. Second, I may act in such a way that I will be approved by other persons or forces so that, in reward for something I have done or because they expect themselves to benefit from me, they will deliver some bit of reality over into my control.

The first way is the way of aggression; the second is the way of appeasement. These two strategies belong necessarily to the life of sin. Since my actuality depends on my having something with my name on it, something in my possession and control to give me an identity, I must constantly work to get something in my control, something in my domination. Sometimes, therefore, I must live by aggression and seize what I need for my identity from others. At other times I must live by appeasement and either earn or wheedle from others what I must possess.

Finally, there is a last law. I must defend what I possess, what I hold as my identity, against the encroachment of others. I project onto them the same kind of identity by which I live, and I know very well what they are struggling to possess. I must work very carefully with them so that our mutual striving to possess does not destroy us all. Consequently, I must work for some compromise where all of us have as many possessions as possible (provided there are not too many shortages). I have a boundary which marks the domain of my reality. I must work constantly to keep others from breaking across my boundary and dispossessing me.

Here we come to the significance of death in the life of sin. Paul says that to be in sin is to be under the domain of death. Why is that? Death here means *to lose our life*. But what does "lose" mean in the perspective of sin? Lose means to be dispossessed, to have the things that are ours, that stand in our possession, that bear our name, and that give us our identity taken from us. That is death. In the perspective of sin death occurs when the boundary that marks off our reality from everything else in the world is totally emptied of everything within it. Death is when our bodies dissolve into the ground or into the air, when our possessions pass to others, when our deeds and our names are forgotten, when nothing exists as belonging to us and thus as giving content, as giving reality, to our identity.

Obviously, death, in this sense, is exclusively a function of our trying to live by means of possessing ourselves, by holding onto ourselves, by having disposal over the resources and content of our own identity. So far as we reject living as a needy and hungry creature who is constantly given being by God, so far as we see our identity as wholly in terms of a reality which we can have and which we can securely label with our own name, we live under the dominion of death; we live under the dominion of dispossession. We live in terror of death, of having this bit of reality which we call ourselves, taken from us. Our whole existence is controlled by that terror.

More important, we discover that life is *taken away from us*—a little each day and finally altogether—for God will not be mocked. God has not established us so that we can forever succeed in securing for ourselves a real identity that denies him as our God and refuses him our gratitude. We can never succeed in making our reality our own. So far as we live out of a sinful identity, we shall live under the law of dispossession, of deprivation, and of death. We shall live to discover that all our having is eventually and totally defeated.

What wages do we receive when we seek a sinful kind of identity? The wages are death, or rather the wages are a life whose inner law is death. And who is ultimately responsible for delivering us over to this death? Who is it that empties and destroys our identity by dispossession? God. God is the enemy of all life by possession. God is the death-giver. Consequently, there is something a little bizarre when Christians, out of panic at the prospect of dispossession, at the prospect of losing their sinful identity, turn to the God of Jesus Christ to help them keep their possessions a little longer.

Now if death is the inner law of sinful identity, then, in the light of Jesus Christ, the bronze dream can only be seen to be a lie. For the bronze dream seeks glory in terms of the being and the life which we possess. It seeks fulfillment in sinful identity. It tries to fabricate an illusory world where the technique of having frees us from death. But bronze life is only an illusion. In God's creation all identity by possession will be taken away. It therefore belongs under the lordship of death.

We cannot speak of sin simply in a personal and individual way. Life by sinful identity partakes of a way of being which extends beyond the human scene and pervades the world as well. What is the center, the real key, to sinful identity? It is the act of possession, the act of making oneself and the resources needed for oneself one's own. This act can be described with another term: *domination*. If I can hold onto myself as my own, as something I really possess and really control, then I am dominating myself. I am the Lord of myself. A sinful kind of identity surely requires aggression or appeasement; it requires defenses against others and against the threat of death as final dispossession. But fundamentally, a sinful kind of identity consists in the act of domination. I am because there is some section of reality which I own, which bears my name and I truly own it; it truly bears my name because I dominate it completely, because it is an instrument of my identity and my will, in short, because it is *my creature*.

In the New Testament Satan is the power of domination. Satan is that characteristic of reality in which reality tries to be by virtue of taking some section of reality and making it its own. The third temptation in Matthew is an extraordinary presentation of the power of domination. Satan takes Jesus up to a high mountain and shows him all the kingdoms of the world. He says to Jesus, "All these I will give you, if you will fall down and worship me" (Matt. 4:9). I will give you these; I will put your name on them, so to speak. I will support your sinful kind of identity, if you worship me. That is, if you honor my domination, if you let me own you, I'll let you own the world. The law of Satan is existence by possession and by domination. Part of the meaning of the new identity in Jesus, the identity which is constantly being received, depends on being convinced that God is not interested in dominating, but in nourishing. The difference between the God of Jesus Christ and of Satan, then, is between a god whose power nourishes and a god whose power dominates. Here we see most clearly the two conditions which Paul calls sin and living-to-God.

But why is the movement from one condition to another a matter of dying with Jesus? How is Jesus' death different from the usual death which is the wages of sin? Instead of simply frustrating our effort to live out of ourselves on the basis of the reality which we possess, why does this death destroy all the power of that old identity and make us ready for the new life? Because in Jesus' death, death goes all the way. It destroys not just the actual possession of being, but the roots of the possessiveness. Or more accurately, in the death of Jesus the way of sinful identity is shown to be what it is: a pretense, a lie, an impossibility.

What propels people to possess? Their *fear of death*, their fear that their identity will be taken from them. They measure their death by looking at themselves, and they measure their life by looking at themselves. On the cross Jesus is maximally pressured to resort to sinful identity. He is pressured by the desertion of his friends. He is pressured by the agony of his body. He is pressured by the desertion of God. In all this dispossession, Jesus is tempted to defend himself and to preserve himself by some act of possession. But he does not fall to that temptation. He does not act to hold onto life, to preserve some segment of being under his control and with his name. Rather, Jesus commends his life, his pneuma, into the hands of his Father. He remains faithful to his ecstatic identity.

FOLLOW ME

Unless we can die with Jesus, unless that radical undoing can occur in us, unless all the roots of this old kind of identity can be abolished, we cannot take on an ecstatic identity of gratitude and joy. The first step in becoming a child of Christ involves a being undone, a losing of the only identity we have ever known. It is, therefore, no accident that Paul speaks of the Christian way as one of fear and trembling (Phil. 2:12). From the viewpoint of the only kind of identity which humans know in sin, life with God seems like death because it involves our possessing nothing to secure our identity. It involves an open poverty that is always waiting to receive.

In the Synoptic Gospels this way of death with Jesus is indicated by a very interesting phrase, which the German scholar Eduard Schweizer has studied. It is the phrase, "follow me."[1] The Synoptics put great emphasis on the fact that Jesus calls his disciples to "follow me." When Jesus calls them to follow him the point becomes clear: following Jesus breaks old ties. First, Jesus calls his followers to break with their occupations. They do not follow Jesus and maintain fishing. Matthew leaves his tax collecting; Peter leaves his boat. Second, Jesus calls his followers to break from their possessions. Remember he says to the rich young man: "Go, sell what you possess and give to the poor . . . and come follow me" (Matt. 19:21). Third, he calls them to break from their family relations. The disciples leave their families, and in response to Jesus' call, one man explains that he must first go bury his father. Jesus says to him: "Follow me and leave the dead to bury their own dead" (Matt. 8:22).

Last and most important, Jesus calls his followers to break from their own selves. "If any man would come after me, let him deny himself and take up his cross and follow me. For whoever would save his life will lose it, and whoever loses his life for my sake will find it" (Matt. 16:24–25).

Those whom Jesus calls are even required to break with themselves. They are required to deny themselves, to lose their lives, for Jesus' sake. They are required to let go of their old identities. Matthew's version of this saying puts it much more concisely: "He who does not take his cross and follow me is not worthy of me" (Matt. 10:38). Self-denial, losing one's life, is involved in taking up Jesus' cross. To follow Jesus requires us to take up our cross.

We must not interpret the phrase "follow me" to mean "follow the principles by which Jesus lives, follow the law of love and all that stuff." That is too abstract. To follow Jesus means to follow his concrete path and that path leads to the cross. To follow Jesus is to die with him and let go the only identity we have. As I see it, when Paul speaks of our dying with Christ so that we may be raised with Christ, he simply states what the Synoptic Gospels name as "follow me," follow Jesus.

THE RESURRECTION

The resurrection is not the gift of a being that will never be taken away from us. If it were, the resurrection would be the restoration of ourselves to sin. It may be a great shock to many people, but the resurrection is ecstatic identity, not possessed identity. The resurrection discredits one fearful possibility—that perhaps there is some fatality in the world, or some historical agency, some cosmic necessity or some other power which will disengage us from God's constituting love, which will establish itself as the source of our identity, and which will thus give us an identity that will be marked by loss, disintegration, and death.

In this context the New Testament points to the suffering and victimization which Jesus endures. Jesus' death shows the efforts of society, of the natural processes, and of the Satanic forces to dispose of him. Jesus' death is their effort to define his identity in their terms, by proving that their rejection of him is his end. This dispossession, their being able to take from him, is indeed his extermination. Therefore, the event of resurrection shows that neither historical force, nor social structure, nor natural necessity, nor cosmic supernatural power can possess and be the origin and content of human identity. Nothing can displace God's own constituting activity. The resurrection means that God's constituting activity does not cease when we no longer share our received being with this world. Our identity, as received from God, is not limited to the present or to the horizons of present experience; only *the being in our possession* is so limited. The being we have from God is as wide as God's own love.

Paul states this situation in a striking way:

> 'We are being done to death for thy sake all day long,' as Scripture says; 'we have been treated like sheep for slaughter'—yet, in spite of all, overwhelming victory is ours through him who loved us. For I am convinced that there is nothing in death or life, in the realm of spirits or superhuman powers, in the world as it is or the world as it shall be, in the forces of the universe, in heights or depths—nothing in all creation that can separate us from the love of God in Christ Jesus our Lord. (Rom. 8:36–39, NEB).

In other words, God's constituting activity is taken to be totally reliable. Death as the loss of possessed being no longer means the end, no longer means extermination or debilitation or mutilation.

In Jesus, God separates us from ourselves. We are not the being that has already been conferred on us, the being which we can mismanage so as to be condemned by the law, or the being which worldly forces can crush and take from us. Our identity has become ecstatic, and God, from whom it constantly issues, never ceases to love. God's giving is not a response to our possessed reality, nor is it in hazardous conflict with other powers. This giving issues wholly and solely out of God's self, out of free loving. And that ground for identity is as inexhaustible as the being of God.

It should now be clear that the meaning of Jesus is not the elimination of death, but rather the reconstitution of identity such that death loses its sting. According to one tradition, during his crucifixion Jesus said, "Father, into thy hands I commit my spirit" (Luke 23:46). This cannot mean: "Father, I have been by virtue of my own reality, but now at death when my reality is being taken from me, I turn to you and ask that after this dispossession you may return some kind of being to me. 'Into your hands I commit my spirit' is a strategy for getting something back into my hands." This death-focused use of God does not apply. Rather, "commending myself into your hands" represents the center and heart of Jesus' identity all through his existence. It represents the center and heart of his identity as the Son of God. It is the center of his "I am."

Such is the structure of ecstatic identity and the new being which we have through Jesus. But to secure this ecstatic identity, we must let go of our old familiar kind of identity; we must be undone and dissolved away; we must let ourselves die; we must be willing to become receivers, receivers of ourselves. This death is not a dreadful enemy in the perspective of Jesus Christ. On the contrary, it is the blessing without which we cannot know the love of God or the fullness of gratitude. It is a *death which brings life*. This is the first transformation or alteration of the meaning of death in the light of Christ.

NOTE

1. Eduard Schweizer, *Lordship and Discipleship* (Naperville, Ill.: A. R. Allenson, 1960).

4

In Christ the Worship of the Father Involves—Death

In the last chapter I reflected upon a new kind of identity, a new way of being. Perhaps we could call it a *receiving without having*, a constant receiving. Perhaps the image for that kind of identity is the image of begging hands. If we possess what we need (especially our identity), then we cannot receive it, nor be grateful for it. We have it, we hold it, and that holding makes us real. In possessing, we are not moved by our neediness beyond ourselves. In other words, we live locked up in ourselves. Prayer as beseeching is constitutive of human existence according to the new identity. It is, however, important to recognize that the aspect of constant receiving applies to every level of human reality.

In the United States we often hear that the inadequacy of possession applies only to worldly and material goods, that through Jesus Christ we have access to unfailing spiritual possessions and may acquire strength, love, and heavenly knowledge that will never fail us. People commonly believe that God's grace will fill us with the possession of certain spiritual powers by which we can maintain our sense of spiritual security in time of trouble.

This belief is, I think, quite false. In the kingdom of God no one is related to any good by way of possession. There is simply no such thing as *possession*. We do not possess ourselves; we constantly *receive* ourselves and *expend* ourselves. We do not possess strength or righteousness or knowledge; we constantly receive them and expend them. And if we try to make any of God's blessings something we possess and have at our disposal, then

61

it will not be long before circumstances will bring us to a situation where our possessions—our possessed faith, possessed love, or possessed piety—prove inadequate. Once again, we are forced back into the condition of spiritual poverty.

SIGN OF THE MANNA

Most unnerving is the realization that we own *nothing* in ourselves to hold onto in the presence of God. At Calvary Jesus cried out, "My God, my God, why have you abandoned me." At this last horizon, Jesus has no spiritual resources or powers to grasp in order to maintain himself in the presence of God. Here he stands forth as a warning to us all against the illusion of spiritual possession. Those who take up the cross of Christ move into *need and dependence*; they do not move toward the acquisition of any spiritual possessions. All human existence, therefore, stands under the sign of the manna which, according to Exodus 16, appears each morning from the dew to nourish the Israelites in the wilderness. Each family can gather as much as they want for that day, but any that is saved over until the next morning becomes full of maggots and stinks. The manna cannot be possessed ahead of time; it can only be received anew each morning.

So it is with all the blessings that nourish and sustain life, including Christian faith, Christian hope, and Christian love. If we try to possess these, if we try to save for tomorrow whatever of these strengths we have received today, they will rot and stink, and tomorrow will prove totally unreliable. By no act of possession can we ever successfully escape from the posture of beseeching toward God, can we ever excuse ourselves at any level of our being from that comprehensive petition in the Lord's Prayer, "Give us this day, on this day, and for this day, our daily bread."

There is nothing inherently wrong with the goods or values, property or virtues that we have. What is wrong is our effort to possess them and to imagine that in any emergency it is only to ourselves and to possessions that we need to turn to have available, ahead of time within our control or ownership, whatever we may require for every contingency. Money in the bank, water in the reservoir, blood plasma in the hospital, and expertise at the other end of the telephone—everywhere, life itself witnesses to the failure of the technique of having. A young man strains to acquire some skill; when he secures it, however, he finds that he's employed by institutions he hardly understands, for purposes of profit and power that he cannot fully accept. When parents have a child taken from them—killed by an irresponsible driver or destroyed by a war that seems senseless or sent to prison for the possession of drugs or driven to aimless wandering by the despair that has no voice—do we imagine that these parents actually possess some riches to nourish them in this devastation? Of course not, because never before could they have imagined for themselves this kind of neediness.

Consider the prospects facing a suburban housewife whom many of us might know. Who can measure the interior boredom and sense of meaninglessness which may grow in her in her mechanized kitchen? One of her children is finishing high school and the other is in junior high. As yet she has found no new direction for her work. Without special training or a tolerance for menial routine, she has not been able to compete with younger women for positions. The pattern of getting involved in mass media causes—poverty, the peace movement, ecology—has become so obviously futile that she cannot pretend her contribution means anything. Her shopping sprees no longer hold excitement, and more frequently now, she finds a drink necessary during the day. This collapse in her life has developed so imperceptibly that as yet it has made no visible mark, and even her husband is unaware of its scope. All her moral training as a self-sufficient, affluent human being now conditions her to evade or to deny her destitution, so that she is incapable of even naming her true distress. She is on the verge of a breakdown. Yet it is simply not the case that there is something available, some insight of a psychiatrist or some belief of a church or some enthusiasm in a dose of drugs which she needs only to secure into her possession in order to make herself emotionally affluent again.

Can anyone measure the destitution between some husbands and wives, between some parents and children? Ravages are everywhere, from the battlefield and ghetto to the board meeting and marriage bedroom. Unquestionably the most compelling challenge to the American gospel of having is posed by the aged. As people grow old, it becomes more and more unnatural for them to sustain their lives and their sense of being human by having riches. To grow old means to enter a stage of life where possessions and skills are only burdens, a stage where poverty becomes wholly natural. The gospel of having does not succeed here anymore than in other situations.

We can express the pervasive failure of the technique of having in a very simple way: *Human need, that is, the experience of need in actual concrete situations, surpasses all resources;* no amount of possessions will give us what we need ahead of time. The life of every individual and of every community is an endless discovery of new forms and new levels of need, is the endless opportunity for new dimensions of beseeching. Take any swinger, take anyone who appears secure and covered with affluent self-assurance—skin smooth, eyes firm, hands strong, and life under control. Just scratch his or her surface and beneath you will find so much distrust and anxiety, such poverty of values and goals, so much secret suffering.

Jesus Christ gives us a new kind of identity where possessions have no place. The consequences are clear. Paul expresses it vividly enough. He asks, "What have you that you did not receive? If then you received it, why do you boast as if it were not a gift?" (1 Cor. 4:7). In living out of the new identity given by Jesus, Paul sees clearly one of its most important features: all glory belongs to God, and we have only to live in the kingdom of God's love. But in Paul's interpretation, we move into this new identity through Jesus only because of the power and the effect of his dying and of our dying with him. By this process, Jesus frees us from ourselves, that is, from finding our being and our identity by holding onto some bit of reality as our own.

Paul puts it this way in 2 Corinthians 5: "we have reached the conclusion that one man died for all and therefore all mankind has died" (2 Cor. 5:14, NEB). The old kind of identity has been shattered, dissolved, irrevocably discredited. Christ's death represents, in a mythic way, the actual dissolution of having for all humans. Paul continues, "His purpose in dying for all was that [people], while still in life, should cease to live for themselves, and should live for him who for their sake died and was raised to life." "With us, therefore," he goes on, "worldly standards [in my language, the standards of existence by possession] have ceased to count in our estimate of any [person]: even if they once counted in our understanding of Christ, they do so no longer" (2 Cor. 5:15–16, NEB).

Paul himself once looked upon Christ from the perspective of the old kind of identity. Because Christ was killed, Paul had believed that Jesus could not possibly be the Messiah, the Son of God. In this way he had once understood Christ by worldly standards. But it is not only Christ that is disclosed as being real in the new way, as constantly receiving from God's giving; Paul continues: "When anyone is united to Christ, there is a new [creation]; the old order has gone [has died with Christ], and a new order has already begun" (2 Cor. 5:17, NEB).

Our lives as recipients and the basic posture of beseeching and receiving in which we are constituted by Jesus Christ are not the whole story of ourselves in the kingdom of God. The sentence by Paul just quoted points up another side of our existence. We cease to live for ourselves and we live for him who for our sake died and was raised to life. Receiving is not all there is to living. To live is *to live for*; that is, living is to act. Therefore, alongside the new identity where we constantly receive ourselves from God, Jesus Christ also gives us a new kind of activity, an activity in accord with that identity. Activity takes a new shape; we do not live for ourselves but for him who died and rose for our sake.

This new kind of activity, this living for Jesus Christ is portrayed in a passage in the Gospel of John. In chapter 12, John writes:

> Among those who went up to worship at the festival were some Greeks. They came to Philip, who was from Bethsaida in Galilee, and said to him, 'Sir, we should like to see Jesus.' So Philip went and told Andrew, and the two of them went to tell Jesus. Then Jesus replied: 'The hour has come for the Son of Man to be glorified. In truth, in very truth I tell you, a grain of wheat remains a solitary grain unless it falls into the ground and dies; but if it dies, it bears a rich harvest. The man who loves himself is lost, but he who hates himself in this world will be kept safe for eternal life. If anyone serves me, he must follow me; where I am, my servant will be. Whoever serves me will be honored by my Father. 'Now my soul is in turmoil, and what am I to say? Father, save me from this hour. No, it was for this that I came to this hour. Father, glorify thy name.' A voice sounded from heaven: 'I have glorified it, and I will glorify it again.' The crowd standing by said it was thunder, while others said, 'An angel has spoken to him.' Jesus replied, 'This voice spoke for your sake, not mine. Now is the hour of judgement for this world; now shall the Prince of this world be driven out. And I shall draw all [people] to myself, when I am lifted up from the earth.' This he said to indicate the kind of death he was to die (John 12:20–33, NEB).

This very dense passage says five different things about Jesus' death. First, in Jesus' death, Jesus is glorified, even as a grain of wheat brings forth a rich harvest by its dying. Second, in Jesus' death, we find eternal life. Those who hate themselves in this world and follow Jesus, that is, who die with Jesus, will be kept safe for eternal life; they will share in the glory of the Father. Third, in Jesus' death, this glorification of Jesus and of us is by the Father. Jesus does not glorify himself; he is glorified. We do not honor ourselves; we are honored. Whoever serves Jesus and follows him and dies with him will be honored by the Father. Fourth, in Jesus' death, the Father is glorified. "What am I to say? Father, save me from this hour. No . . . Father, glorify thy name." If Jesus' death is glorification of the Son of Man and of us, it is also the glorification of the Father. Fifth and finally, in Jesus' death, all people are drawn to him. He judges the world; he overcomes and expels the power of evil.

Note here John's pun: "I shall draw all [people] to myself, when I am lifted up." What is lifted up? The resurrection? No, "This he said to indicate the kind of death he was to die." (We might guess that already at the time John was writing Christians were beginning to look to the resurrection in order to avoid Jesus' death—a pattern that has not disappeared for the church.) Note that Jesus draws all people, just when you would think he would offend all people: *when he dies.*

GLORY

This is a very loaded passage. The central strand, however, is expressed by the word "glory." Jesus' glory glorifies those who serve him, who share in his life and glory. The Father glorifies his name and those structures and powers which oppose this glory are overcome. What John presents here is an account of glory. Now what is glory? Glory is that which we worship. Glory and worship belong together. Worship is the act of responding to glory, and glory is the act which elicits worship. There have been periods in the history of Christianity when the raison d'être of the church and of Christian existence was thought to be one thing only, the worship offered to God. The earliest centuries of the church, from which our New Testament writings come, was such a period.

This passage in John invites reflection on Christian worship and its connection to glory and the death of Jesus. The term "worship" comes from the Old English term "worth-ship." It means rendering to any person that to which their worth or their worthiness entitles them. "Your worship" is still an expression within English law. God is entitled to a worship that has no limits. What God is, apart from what God does to and for creatures, is supremely worthy and therefore supremely worshipful. Worship arises in us, not when we reflect on God's goodness toward us and then try to decide what we owe in return (my whole self, say); but worship arises when we reflect on what God is in God's own perfections and being, and then ask with what offering such perfection should be honored. This supreme worship is called in the New Testament *latreia*. The key Old Testament text is Deut. 6:13. In Matthew, Jesus says to Satan, "Begone, Satan; Scripture says, 'You shall do homage to the Lord your God and worship him alone'" (Matt. 4:10, NEB). "Worship" here means *latreia*, what is due to God alone.

In the New Testament, the word *latreia* is used extensively. Four passages provide a sense of the centrality of the term. The first is from Luke 1, the prophecy of Zechariah:

> Praise to the God of Israel! For he has turned to his people, saved them and set them free. . . . Such was the oath he swore to our father Abraham, to rescue us from enemy hands, and to grant us, free from fear, to worship him with a holy worship, with uprightness of heart, in his presence, our whole life long (Luke 1:68, 73–75, NEB).

In short, God rescues us. For what purpose? So we may worship him.

A second passage is from Hebrews 9:

> For if the blood of goats and bulls and the sprinkled ashes of a heifer have power to hallow those who have been defiled and restore their external purity, how much greater is the power of the blood of Christ; he offered himself without blemish to God, a spiritual and eternal sacrifice; and his blood will cleanse our conscience from the deadness of our former ways and fit us for the *latreia* of the living God (Heb. 9:13–14, NEB).

We are cleansed. For what purpose? For worship.

A third passage from Revelation 7 looks to the eschaton, to the completion of all things:

> Then he said to me, 'These are the men who have passed through the great ordeal; they have washed their robes and made them white in the blood of the Lamb. That is why they stand before the throne of God and [give *latreia* to] him day and night in his temple; and he who sits on the throne will dwell with them. They shall never again feel hunger or thirst . . . (Rev. 7:14–16, NEB).

The whole content then of the goal of human existence becomes *latreia*.

Finally, the fourth passage turns not to the end of all things, but toward the beginning: the worship of God was lost when the human race turned and broke from God. Here in Romans 1 Paul writes of those who have turned from God:

> Because they have bartered away the true God for a false one, and have

offered reverence and worship to created things instead of to the Creator, who is blessed forever; amen (Rom. 1:25, NEB).

I gather that this last phrase is what Paul means by an instance of true worship—blessing and praising God as the creator of all things. This *latreia* has been lost in the disruption of humanity's relationship to God.

In the New Testament worship becomes the comprehensive sense of human existence. It becomes the way of understanding human existence in the light of Jesus. Human existence is not to achieve, not to run, not to live. It is to worship, and it is for the restoration of worship that Jesus has come. But if we consider worship as an honoring of God's worthiness, we realize immediately that this view poses a problem. God's worthiness is such that we are totally unable to give it adequate honor. Even all creatures together cannot render unto God the honor that befits his perfection, his worthiness. Here we confront a universal problem in all religions. In many religions there is a specific procedure for making our offerings worthy of divinity—*consecration*. A gift from humanity must be transformed by divinity itself into something worthy of deity. Consecration is that procedure given by the divinity.

It is really shocking to notice that in many of our Protestant churches the sense of consecration has disappeared. For reasons perhaps best reflected in Britain, the offering of money is somehow thought to be sufficient. (I say perhaps best reflected in Britain because, as far as I know, Britain is the only country that has holidays to our modern god; it has bank holidays!) In any case, for the church of the bronze people, there seems to be no sense of any need to consecrate money. There is no sense that money is degrading to God, is unworthy of God, is a blasphemous offering. Beneath the cross where Jesus offered himself to the Father, the money is brought up without any sense of utter inadequacy. The problem of consecration is the fundamental problem of worship. What do I offer? How can my offering be transformed so that it should not be rejected?

For the New Testament there is a clear sense that humanity has lost all intention to honor God. Humanity has forgotten God and now worships only creatures of the world or creatures of our diseased minds. Where is the worship of God restored? For the New Testament writings through and through, the meaning of Jesus Christ is that he restores our worship of God. Hebrews 9 says this plainly: "He offered himself without blemish to

God," a perfect sacrifice, and through him we become fit for the worship of the living God. Jesus Christ then is the indispensable consecrator. His worship is perfect. We worship only in and through him. For our sake, he honors God adequately and he does so in his dying.

THE HELL OF BOREDOM

Nothing, I suppose, is more obvious today than the way worship has become an increasingly unfamiliar activity. The loss of worship marks a secular society. Its only horizons are those provided by the present immediate world. The idea of honoring some god who is not part of the immediate world seems a bit strange. The further idea of identifying the fulfillment of human existence with such worship seems preposterous and superstitious. Worship is certainly no preoccupation of a secular age. If the secular perspective wants glory, wants that which elicits worship, it insists that that glory be found in our immediate world and not in some transcendent fiction. Yet it is in these exact terms that the worship of God's glory has always been valued. God's glory, religious persons have contended, is infinitely deeper and richer than the glory of anything in the world.

The heritage of a secular age, however, is boredom. The human spirit cannot be satisfied and exalted by the glory, say, of human thought or national sovereignty, of utopian visions or muscular athletics, or even, of self-sacrificing love. These have a kind of glory; they elicit praise; they elicit that sense of the wonderful which is so strong in the human heart. But in each case they are a limited glory. In human thought, in national sovereignty, in utopian visions, in muscular athletics, or in self-sacrificing love, we can always find degrading motives. We are always able to find feeble and incompetent power. We cannot worship any of these with all of our intellectual and moral passion. We cannot find elicited in any of these that sense of awe, that exaltation of which we know we are capable. Somewhere we will be bothered by inadequacy.

More important, however, when people live by possessed identity, they are threatened by worship, by glories and magnitudes which utterly surpass them. Such immensities can smother their sense of their own identity. In this way worship can serve perhaps their self-hatred, their yearning to run away from themselves and to abolish themselves. I often think that many people go into the ministry of loving the unworthy neighbor as a way of running from themselves. Such ministry is always an expression of self-hatred, and such worship becomes rather destructive.

Most people who live and who try to be real by holding onto themselves do not want glory—hence, the intolerable boredom into which they become so easily locked. They cannot be open to new input, especially the input of glory which will only make them dissatisfied with the stale and limited proportions of their own identity. They tend to be limited to what they can possess, and in that limited condition they know the hell of boredom. To be joyful in the worship of the living God is to be redeemed from all boredom. But this is also to abandon one's identity by self-possession. It is a grim choice: either the worship of a living God and the concomitant loss of identity by self-possession or identity by self-possession and the consequent ordeal of boredom.

It is interesting to consider the view of heaven as a place where everyone securely has his or her own identity for ever and ever and ever and ever—a view of heaven often attributed to Christianity. Such a vision makes heaven seem like a place of intolerable boredom. In most people this view of heaven can only induce a strong feeling of nausea. A heaven where we possess ourselves and live for ourselves would be a place from which God and his glory have been completely locked out. Such are the secular heavens for which most of us live.

GLORY IN DEATH

Now, the Gospel of John is totally preoccupied with the themes of glory, of fulfilled life, and of realized worship. John identifies these themes with the death of Jesus. However, the death of Jesus can only be understood when we know who Jesus is. The first part of John's Gospel concentrates on showing us who Jesus is; the second part focuses on the significance of Jesus' dying. John sums up everything that can be said about the identity of Jesus in one phrase, he is "from the Father." He not only comes from the Father in a sequential sense. All that he has and is comes from the Father. The Father gives the Son of Man his knowledge, his purposes in will, his authority in judgment, and above all, his life. The Son has life in himself, not from himself, but from the Father. Yet, from the Father, the Son has life, life within himself. In all of this, John presents Jesus as living by what I have called an ecstatic identity—a being not by virtue of anything that is his own, but a being by virtue of what the Father continually communicates to him.

Like the letters of Paul, John points out that Jesus' way of existing is faithful to this identity. Because Jesus comes from the Father, continually constituted by the Father, Jesus is and does nothing in terms of his independent selfhood. He does not do his own will; he does his Father's will. Why? Because in every corner of his being, he is from the Father. In John's Gospel, Jesus says, "God is the source of my being, and from him I come. I have not come of my own accord; he sent me" (John 8:42, NEB). Jesus does not act out of his own authority. He says, in fact, "I do nothing of my own authority." Why? "In all that I say, I have been taught by my Father" (John 8:28, NEB). All that Jesus knows comes continually from the Father. He does not act by himself because, as he says, "My aim is not my own will, but the will of him who sent me" (John 5:30, NEB). Jesus does not even speak his own words. He says, "It is the Father who dwells in me doing his own work" (John 14:10, NEB). The overwhelming conclusion is clear and succinct: do not believe in Jesus but believe in the Father who sent the Son.

In the Gospel of John, Jesus lives in total conformity with his identity as constantly coming to him from the Father and as never belonging to him. John uses the term "glory" to crystalize all of this. Jesus has glory but it comes to him from the Father. Jesus shares in that higher radiance which draws forth from us the response of praise and wonder. He does not glorify himself. "If I glorify myself," he says, "that glory of mine is worthless. It is the Father who glorifies me" (John 8:54, NEB). Jesus does not seek people to give him glory. "I do not look to men for honor. . . . I have come accredited by my Father" (John 5:41–43, NEB). In glory, in praise, in worthiness, as in all other features of his being, Jesus derives solely from the Father; in that sense he is "from above." In all things, Jesus gives glory to the Father. He seeks that, in and through himself, we believe and praise only the Father. Therefore, Jesus obeys the Father so that in Jesus his Father's will may be seen and not his own. Jesus offers all of himself to the Father, holding back nothing of his own. In obedience and offering, Jesus gives glory to the Father. For John, Jesus' decisive act of obedience and offering is his laying down of his life.

Here we come to the decisive point—in Jesus' dying the Father is glorified. This must mean that in Jesus' dying the Father is *truly* revealed in glory; for God is revealed only in glory. In other words, by his death Jesus does not praise a God we already know and honor. I don't think John senses that. Rather, Jesus relates us to God in glory in a way that we have never known before. In Jesus' death God glorifies divinity to us. Jesus draws all people to himself and to the glory of his Father. As our acknowledgment of glory, worship is called forth from us in a new way by Jesus' death.

We may now ask the decisive question: what is this glory of the Father? One tradition, still very strong in both Catholic and Protestant communities, claims that we worship God's unique immensity and omnipotence, the transcendent quality of God that marks God as different from creatures. According to this view, in worship we are grasped by God's transcendent otherness; we are caught up out of ourselves in the ungraspable magnificence of an inexhaustible infinitude. The essential character of this worship is contemplation. I contemplate the divine being which exists totally beyond me. Worship then is essentially the role of the spectator.

I believe that the Gospel of John repudiates this tradition of worship. In this Gospel, that in God which draws forth our worship (God's glory) is not God's transcendent infinitude; it is not God's complete identity with its perfect reality. There are two passages where John explicitly identifies a different meaning of glory. First, in chapter 15 Jesus says to his disciples, "This is my Father's glory, that you may bear fruit in plenty and so be my disciples" (John 15:8, NEB). In other words, the dynamic act of bearing fruit, of engendering and communicating life, is the Father's glory. It is also that by which people become identified before God as Jesus' disciples.

The second passage, even more striking, comes from chapter 12 which I quoted earlier. Referring to his death, Jesus says, "The hour has come for the Son of Man to be glorified." Then Jesus gives a curious explanation which identifies glory with the power of bearing fruit, the power of bearing fruit that entails dying. Jesus says, "In very truth I tell you, a grain of wheat remains a solitary grain unless it falls into the ground and dies, but if it dies, it bears a rich harvest" (John 12:23–24, NEB). In short, the Son of Man is glorified because he bears a rich harvest; he bears fruit in plenty. But how does he bear fruit in plenty? How does he communicate beyond himself the identity of life which he receives from the Father? The Son of Man does so like the grain of wheat—by dying.

COMMUNICATION OF LIFE

The image of the grain of wheat represents an astonishing proposal. It construes death as the process of generating and communicating identity in life. In this teaching Jesus interprets his death in terms of the agricultural process of sowing. When a grain of wheat is put into the ground and cracks open, when it releases from itself its own life and reality and dies, only then does it yield a harvest. Here emerges the principle that within the arena of Jesus the act of conferring and nourishing life for others *requires* the loss and expenditure of one's own life. The Gospel of John especially celebrates Jesus' death as the process whereby the new kind of received life and received identity is extended to the human race. Like the grain of wheat which bears fruit by dying, Jesus' dying is the gift to us of the identity he receives from his Father. Jesus says that his death is how we receive his life.

We should examine how John writes about Jesus' actual moment of death. To appreciate John, notice the way Matthew describes the moment in his Gospel, "Jesus gave a loud cry and gave up the *pneuma*," gave up the spirit (Matt. 27:50, au. trans.). When John writes of this, he rejects Matthew's notion of "gave up," as if in the moment of death the *pneuma*, the life, the vital identity of Jesus, were simply lost. Instead of the verb "gave up," John uses the verb "to hand over," *paradidōmi*. New Testament writers use this verb frequently. For example, in the temptation story of Luke 4, Satan says to Jesus that he will "hand over" to Jesus all the kingdoms of the world. In 1 Corinthians 15 when Paul is speaking of the eschaton, he writes that Jesus will "hand over" the kingdom to God the Father.

For John Jesus at his death did not give up the spirit or life which was in himself. He handed it over. To whom? Here is John's account. Jesus is speaking to his mother Mary and the disciple John who are standing beneath him. He is then given a sponge soaked in wine. John writes: "Having received the wine, [Jesus] said, 'It is accomplished.' He bowed his head and [handed over] his spirit" (John 19:30, NEB). When the verb "hand over" is given prominence, the whole sentence takes on a new meaning. What is the completion of Jesus' work? What does he refer to as being accomplished? Not his dying, but rather that which occurs through his dying, the handing over of his *pneuma*, his life, to others. Jesus hands over to others, to Mary and John and the human race, the identity he receives from the Father. Why does John say that Jesus bows his head? Because he hands his spirit, his vital identity, over to Mary and John who are standing beneath him. In John's account Jesus' death stands out as an event of the *communication of life* to the specific figures beneath him, to Mary and John, and through them to the human race.

In the Gospel of John, however, the most important symbol of Jesus' death as the communication of life is the bread and wine of the Eucharist. Jesus' death is symbolized by our eating bread and our drinking wine. Why? Is it because these sacraments represent Jesus' dying? No. It is because these sacraments represent the taking of life. They represent Jesus' death, not as death in a dreadful sense, but as the communication and nourishment of life in us, as the handing over to us and taking in by us of the pneumatic identity, the life-full identity which he lived.

Jesus does not die, period. He lays down his life to nourish us. We eat his body and we drink his blood. Like the plants and animals that nourish and constitute us each day, he nourishes us by handing over his own life, his own pneumatic identity. This is the glory which Jesus receives at his crucifixion. He communicates to us the newness of life that is within him. His glory then is to bear fruit, to produce a rich harvest, to engender new life. But remember the Father does not glorify Jesus alone; the Father also glorifies his name, that is, discloses the quality of his reality which should draw forth our worship.

What is shown here? God's transcendence? God's immense infinitude? The utter difference which marks God off from all mortal creatures? Not at all. The Father, as revealed by Jesus in his dying, is the origin and principle of this glory, this vitality of bearing fruit and engendering life, this vitality which we meet in Jesus. The glory of God the Father is identical in kind to the glory of Jesus' sacrificial death. God is to be worshiped, not because God is absolute, but because *God engenders and communicates life.*

In the history of the Christian church there was one moment when the glory of God arose as a decisive problem. This was at a point which called forth the Council of Nicaea. It was the issue between Athanasius, on the one hand, and Arius, on the other. Arius insisted that God alone was God and that God was to be worshiped by the Christian church because God was absolute, because in Arius's magnificent term God was "the alone with the alone." Athanasius insisted that God was to be worshiped because God was a Father who engendered a Son, and because God was a Father who engendered a Son in whom all his glory was shared. The fact that the Son was equal to the Father and could be worshipped as fully divine, this meant that there was no part of divine reality that was not communicated. Through and through, God was a communicating being.

The Christian worships not the absoluteness of God but the *fecundity of God,* the fact that the Father engenders the Son who carries the fullness of divinity. God is not God as superior, as superior to us in holding onto the divine reality. We do not worship God as a self-contained divinity. We worship God for the glory of the Father, a glory which consists in bearing fruit. That is the meaning of the cross. We worship God as Father, that is, as one who engenders the Son. We worship God further as one, who not only engenders the Son, but engenders in all of us the same life. Where do we see the glory of God? In the Son. Here the Father is glorified, and fruitful power is the Father's and not the Son's own. Worship then is a response to glory. Where is glory? In Jesus' act of dying. In the act he shares his glory and bestows life, but we worship here the glory of the Father.

In Jesus Christ we see that none of us is simply the life we now receive because we will receive again anew each day. Therefore, in laying down his life, Jesus does not abolish his identity. He does not commit suicide in the sense of acting so as to be nothing. His identity does not depend on and does not consist in the life which he holds onto and the life which he offers. He is by virtue of God, by virtue of God's constant activity to him and with him. Without detriment to his true self, he can give away everything of himself. He can give away everything at his disposal. He can lay down his life and receive it again. Contrary to all the injunctions against suicide, Jesus claims the right to give away everything.

Just as Jesus dies to nourish others, the laying down of life becomes something our freedom can also choose. It becomes a *human moral possibility;* it becomes something not over against life, but within life; it becomes the process of communicating life. But isn't this suicide? Do we have the right to lay down our lives? In John 10, Jesus says: "No one has robbed me of [my life]; I am laying it down of my own free will. I have the right to lay it down . . . this charge I have received from my Father" (John 10:18, NEB). Jesus has the right to die. He rejects the prohibition of suicide.

Suicide is the supreme evil for the old identity by possession. To let go of your life is to lose your being, to lose your identity when your identity is only what you possess. But in this realm of the cross, to lay down life is not to lose identity, because identity does not lie within ourselves; it lies in God's giving. Therefore, to lay down the life we have already received, to lay it down that it may engender life in others, is not to die in the sense of being abolished; it is to die in the sense of generating life.

Clearly, the act of generating life, the act of losing life, is not something that happens momentarily. It is the nature of human existence. All our lives we are expending ourselves, and in expending ourselves we are nourishing in others what we have received. The act of nourishing in others what we have received is to reflect the glory of the Father. It is to reflect the glory of Christ on the cross and is to be honored. The essence of dignity in the Christian arena is to engender life, to engender it in single acts, to engender it in a lifetime of self-expenditure. The act of being honored is the act of becoming poor when that becoming poor involves our expending ourselves that others may be nourished.

In the cross, Jesus is glorified as the Son of Man. He shares in the mystery of vitality; the power of generating life invests him with radiance. So far as we are disciples, so far as we generate life not by giving what we do not need (our extra money, our surplus blood, our needless time), so far as we generate life by giving what we need (by giving the life in us) and through that giving are driven into need ourselves, so far as we do this, we are honored by the Father. The story of Jesus is also our story. So far as we follow Jesus, so far as we live under the shape of his dying and lay down our lives for our neighbors, we are honored by the Father. In that light we honor one another.

Remember, however, that this glory, this honor, this dignity are not that of possessed identity; they are not to keep myself alive, to keep myself real, to hold onto my own identity. I am free to give myself away, provided that what I give is not anything that I do not need, provided that what I give is the substance of my own life. In Jesus Christ, therefore, we have the freedom to love; we have the freedom to love by laying down our life. The new kind of identity which Jesus brings involves this new life, a freedom absolutely unthinkable to those who live by possession. The freedom to love is the freedom to do what Jesus did on the cross, the freedom to give ourselves away.

5

In Christ the Love of the Neighbor Involves—Death

In the last chapter I focused on that remarkable text in John 12. I simply tried to take seriously its claims. It asserts that the death of Jesus is his glorification, is our glorification (provided we share in it), and is his Father's glorification (a really remarkable claim). I have tried to make sense out of it with the notion that life is a matter of bearing fruit outside of oneself in others. It is a matter of nourishing others, of generating and of maintaining, of preserving and of enriching life beyond ourselves. So if the notion of the seed that dies and bears fruit is the real key to the power of God and the glory of God as revealed in Jesus at his death, then this key becomes the criterion for what life is.

Here we have a very severe judgment on the more normal sense that life is what we have inside ourselves. Normally, to decide whether we are alive we do not look outside of ourselves to find out if we are nourishing and generating life. We look into ourselves to find out how strong and healthy and vital we are. But the notion of the seed that dies demands an extraordinary *redirection* of the sense of life. Now to know if anyone is alive, we do not look at them; look beyond them to the mode of their expenditures and the life that they nourish and preserve beyond themselves. Admittedly, this idea is very primitive; it is not very sophisticated, not intellectual. It is a very basic idea that *life is the generation of life* and that a life which does not generate is sterile. As Athanasius used to say when he was fighting Arius, the unitarian god of Arius is a sterile god and as such, a dead god because that god only has life within the divine self.

I have tried to tie together this idea about life with the third chapter's discussion of Paul by observing that God does not have a possessed identity; God does not have an identity locked into the divine self. The glory of God that calls forth our worship is not God's absoluteness, that is, not an identity perfected by secure possession of it. God is not God because God holds the divine identity and does not let anyone else have it. That is the mark of Satan. God is God because God *shares* that identity, the Father with the Son, and through the Son, the Father with us. Here is a very different image of the meaning of God as the foundation of the universe and, therefore, of our own lives. God then is the power to communicate life. God's will is the will to communicate life. In this regard we believe that Jesus in his dying is doing God's will and is revealing God's wonderfulness. Therefore, it really is Good Friday! You don't have to wait for Sunday; it's really Good Friday. There are dreadful aspects, the human barbarity, but these dreadful aspects are not at the center. And to us the Eucharist, the bread and wine which we eat and drink, represents to us Christ's death as life-giving, self-giving expenditure. That is why in our communities we *eat* to represent his death.

THE NEW WORSHIP

You can see, then, that I am especially concerned to attack the idea of God as a self-contained absolute. But I am also concerned to attack the kind of worship that this absolute and self-contained God calls forth. Here worship is losing ourselves in God or being swallowed up in him by his immensity. Worship is the attitude where there is nothing but God and all creatures have vanished from my horizon.

In contrast to the worship of a god who is so big I just lose myself and where my essential role in worship is as a spectator of his magnificence, a second model looks at the cross as the perfection of worship. The cross is not Jesus being lost in God, is not Jesus offering himself to God by giving himself up to God. Jesus gives himself up; he gives himself away, but not to God. He gives himself away to us. On the cross, Jesus shares in God's glory, is himself empowered by and is the bearer of God's power to engender life. This is God's power, but Jesus freely lives by it in expending his life for us. Jesus' worship, then, consists, not in doing something different from communicating life to the lost children of God, but in how he communicates this life. His worship consists in his doing all this for his Father's glory. Jesus makes clear by his words and actions that the glory which glorifies him is from beyond him, is from God. He makes clear that even in the act which glorifies him, which radiates him with supreme power, even in the act of expending himself to nourish us with life, even there he is only a receiver, not an originator, not an owner: in New Testament language, even there Jesus is only "a Son."

Worship is not annihilating oneself so that God can be everything. The God disclosed in Jesus' death does not want to be everything. This God abominates being everything. This God wills to nourish life, to establish life, and to have life thrive beyond divinity. Worship is a way of performing the activities of generating life, of restoring life, of healing life. It involves acts of obedience to God as God's will and not ours. Worship involves these acts in the knowledge that the power of life-giving comes from God continually and glorifies God always. Worship is for us to love our neighbor as the work of God, just as in the pattern of Jesus' own activity. When we worship we do not stop being creative toward our needy friends and enemies anymore than, in glorifying God, Jesus has to stop extending his life to us and for us. When we worship God, we worship a glory in which we share, in which we stand, by which we are honored.

In worshiping God, there can be no debasing of ourselves, no abolishing of ourselves, no hiding of ourselves. In worshiping God, we do the work of God, but we do it as the work of God. We communicate and expend the life in us to others as an exercise in us, by our free consent, of God's power, as the realization in us of God's will, as the presence in us of God's kingship. Precisely in the lowliness of being receptive, of being only the servants of Christ, we stand on the dignity of ourselves as his heirs, of ourselves being coworkers with God. Loving our neighbors by self-expenditure is the only way we may worship. And worshiping God is the only way in which we can proceed to love our neighbors.

In this connection let me make one observation. If the New Testament understands worship as the content of the eschatological life, then should we not say that self-expenditure even unto death is also a component in that life of heaven? Jesus says, "No one has greater love than this, than to lay down his life for his friend" (John 15:13, au. trans.). The true character of love is self-expenditure, the expending and dispossessing and undoing of oneself for the nourishment of others. This teaching, of course, represents the statement of Jesus' own loving, for he lays down his life to nourish all. Can we really believe that in heaven, in the kingdom of God, in that condition where God's will is done, that there will be no total self-expenditure, no laying down one's life for one's friends, no supreme acts of love? Can we really believe that the highest love is only to be found here in our present life and that in the fullness of God's kingdom, we will only exercise reduced forms of love because there will be no death? Will it be true that in heaven, because we will have some life principle in us, we will be doomed never to give ourselves away to nourish our neighbors, never to expend our lives for our friends? I do not believe this is true.

The kingdom of heaven will be rich in self-expenditure and therefore also rich in the loss of life, in the giving up of life for others, in the giving away of life. Always, of course, life will be restored by God—for death is simply, in this perspective, the essential condition of need in which we wait upon God to give us ourselves. Death, I believe, will not be removed in heaven. What will be removed is the imposition of death, the use of death for terror and hatred, the fear of death, the perverse craving of the people who feel this fear to possess life; this is what will be removed in heaven.

THE GOOD SAMARITAN

In this chapter we will consider a new set of problems, in light of a New Testament parable.

> On one occasion a lawyer came forward to put this test question to [Jesus]: 'Master, what must I do to inherit eternal life?' Jesus said, 'What is written in the Law? What is your reading of it?' He replied, 'Love the Lord your God with all your heart, with all your soul, with all your strength, and with all your mind; and your neighbor as yourself.' 'That is the right answer,' said Jesus; 'do that and you will live.' But [the lawyer] wanted to vindicate himself, so he said to Jesus, 'And who is my neighbor?' Jesus replied, 'A man was on his way from Jerusalem down to Jericho when he fell in with robbers, who stripped him, beat him, and went off leaving him half dead. It so happened that a priest was going down by the same road; but when he saw him, he went past on the other side. So too a Levite came to the place, and when he saw him went past on the other side. But a Samaritan who was making the journey came upon him, and when he saw him was moved to pity. He went up and bandaged his wounds, bathing them with oil and wine. Then he lifted him on his own beast, brought him to an inn, and looked after him there. Next day he produced two silver pieces and gave them to the innkeeper, and said, "Look after him, and if you spend any more, I will repay you on my way

back." Which of these three do you think was neighbor to the man who fell into the hands of robbers?' [The lawyer] answered, 'The one who showed him kindness.' Jesus said, 'Go and do as he did' (Luke 10:25–37, NEB).

This parable confronts us with the incredible contrast between the bronze dream, on the one hand, and the way of Jesus Christ, on the other. Before dealing with the parable, however, let me develop more sharply these two perspectives. The way of Jesus is the way of self-expenditure. He calls us not just to serve each other, but to do so with the ability to die willingly—"Greater love has no person than that." In such actions we share in the glory and power of God. For God the Father is the Lord of that self-expenditure which engenders life, communicates life, and nourishes life. To do that is the content of God's will for human existence, at least as realized by Jesus; to do that is to come upon what I am calling the new kind of identity, to do that because it is God's will and because it exhibits God's kind of power, to do that as someone who constantly receives from God and insists on claiming nothing as his own; to do that through Jesus Christ is to provide God the only worship which is consecrated.

Our efforts to honor God, our worship, is not adequate. It is utterly unworthy of God. But because such efforts of self-expenditure are done in obedience to God and for God's glory, they are consecrated; that is, they are made worthy of God's goodness and perfection by the sacrifice of Christ. The activity of worship then embraces the two aspects of human existence. It embraces the beseeching by which we acknowledge our need constantly to receive. It also embraces the act of self-expenditure by which life is communicated to the dead, sight to the blind, and liberty to the oppressed.

The way of the bronze dream is just the opposite. A person is by way of holding and possessing; persons try to hold and possess their own identity; and they try to hold and possess the resources and supports by which that identity can be sustained. In other words, the bronze way seeks a mode of life which promises maximum security.

When, in the kingdom of Jesus, we live as those who own nothing and who constantly receive from God, when we let ourselves depend fully on God, then our feeling of being safe is grounded in our confidence that God will be reliable in nourishing us, our feeling of being safe consists in our faith in God. But when we live by the bronze dream, our feeling of being safe depends on how well we can hold and possess our identity, on how well the resources to support it are within our control. So far as we do live in this way, we depend on no one and nothing but ourselves and our power to hold on to ourselves and our possessions. Or to put it sharply, we find our identity in what is at our disposal. The bronze way of trying to feel safe has nothing to do with God or with anyone else. I am my own master and I have the *feeling of security*—that resting, that feeling safe, which is grounded in the fact that we possess, that we have under our control and at our bidding whatever we may need.

These then are the two ways. In the one where Jesus rules, death may be the communication of the life which we can receive only from God and can never possess, hold, or nail down as our own. In the way of the bronze people, death is the absolute enemy; death is the final deprivation, the final end of all having and possessing. Death is the most extreme neediness. We no longer possess those potencies that give content to our identity; that is, life and goodness and happiness are no longer a matter of having and possessing. Consequently, death represents the absolute evil. Faith, as confidence in God, is to be safe because of something utterly beyond our control and outside our own horizons. Security is to be safe because of something completely under our control. From the viewpoint of security, faith seems to be an empty and completely insecure activity. But from the point of view of faith, security, as a resting on our own power to master and control, seems to be temporary, feeble, and in the end, useless.

Now we can understand the difference in the two ways in a clearer light. Actually, it is not death itself which is the basic issue. The basic issue rather concerns an essential aspect of our human nature: *the aspect of neediness*. When the bronze dream identifies life and well-being with holding and possessing ourselves and whatever we require, neediness becomes the primary evil. To find within the boundary by which we mark our own reality that we do not have there what we need—this is the root of evil. Death is the final fruit of that evil, the final consequence. But the root is to find neediness within the circle of our own having. Our neediness which forces us to derive and maintain our life from what lies outside of us—this we try to remove. We simply expand the circle that is ourselves and that has our name on it to include whatever we require.

Since we cannot do this privately and individually, we form communities so that the community owns everything we need. We have security;

we ourselves possess and have disposal over everything our existence requires, not privately, but through the community. In this perspective, to need and not to have are the abomination. Death simply proves beyond a shadow of a doubt that neediness without possessions is utterly destructive. So all communities live in order to possess and to have such a source of riches that all neediness may be immediately forestalled.

FAITH TOWARD NEEDINESS

In the kingdom of Jesus, however, in the new kind of identity which he brings, where we are constantly receiving and never holding and possessing, where we are always looking to God for our reality and not to ourselves, here human life is a *resting-in-neediness*, is a neediness that constitutes the character of our relationship to God. In the kingdom of Jesus, in the life of love, a life where we are able to let go of all we have received so that it may go and nourish others, here human activity is a *response to the neediness of others*. And when, in the light of Jesus' cross, I observe how that self-expending love may entail our debt, may involve us in losing all possessed identity, losing all that is within the circle of ourselves, then I am describing the conclusion of human activity as a *movement toward extreme neediness*. In short, in the kingdom of Jesus we always begin with neediness, we always live outward toward neediness, and we always end in neediness.

From the viewpoint of the new creature, evil now appears in two forms. Basically it appears as our trying to suppress within ourselves any hint of our own neediness. But it also appears in our abusing rather than nourishing others who are needy. Both kinds of behavior, however, have the same source. In the first form of evil, where we try to live by our capacity to possess and where we try to remove all traces of neediness in ourselves, we act so that our own neediness will not affect us. In the second form of evil, where we dominate, exploit, and ravage those who are in need, we act so that the neediness of others does not affect or control us. In either case, with the rich as with the oppressed, life is essentially a refusal to be affected by neediness, a refusal to recognize neediness, to respond to neediness, and to rest in neediness.

Why such opposite judgments about neediness? Why, in the one perspective, is it intolerable and dreadful, and in the other, fully acceptable? The difference is the love of God. No, the difference is the God who is essentially the Father, who is engendering and communicating life, who is love. If this God is the Creator and Lord of all reality, then we have no fear of need. That is what this God essentially means. God's perfect love casts out all fear. But if reality is alien, then poverty and neediness represent conditions where we are utterly defenseless against barbarity, mutilation, and loss. In this world there are persons and there are dark structures of the cosmos which seize upon human neediness for purposes of domination, oppression, and victimization. In such actions they stand opposed to God, to the nature of God, to the power of God, and to the will of God. In such actions they confront us as if they really had disposal over human existence, as if their disposition, their exploitation, their destruction were the last words, as if they represented the final power in the universe.

In this way demonic agencies tempt men and women to deny that the Father of Jesus Christ is the true God. They tempt them to construe need as it appears before their action, that is, as something dreadful and pernicious. They seduce people to find their salvation in a flight from neediness. They proclaim death to be their god; they proclaim, by their dread of need, that death is the master of neediness. Through fear of neediness they pay homage to death and not to God. In the second chapter I described the subtle kind of worship of death with its flight from neediness as a very strong trend in our American life.

COURAGE CASTING OUT FEAR

In the churches we must be very careful with the word "faith." The term signifies that we place our confidence in God the Father, that is, in God, the engenderer, in God the life communicator, and in his Son Jesus Christ. Faith signifies that we are one with our own neediness, that we are willing to receive everything each day from God and do not have to possess, that we are free to be needy, free both to receive God's blessings and to bestow all that we have upon our needy neighbor.

But to speak thus of faith makes faith still sound pleasant and easy, and congenial to the bronze dream. We have not yet made explicit the *fear* which must be overcome in faith. We need to indicate the ordeal which faith must endure when it confronts exploitation and victimization, when it confronts the powers that use killing to exalt themselves. In this regard, because all of life is being assaulted by the pseudo-gods of domination, by the gods whose final pretenses to power consist in their ability to kill, faith must have, as its primary form, the virtue of *courage*.

There is no act of trusting in God, as disclosed through Jesus Christ, which is not as such an act of courage, of the courage not to flee from neediness even when that neediness is being exploited by greed, by pride, or by hate. Faith requires courage to join the needy, to comfort them in their affliction, to call them out of their despair, to countermand their fear. In this regard, the act of faith and the loving service that accompanies faith always have the character of courage. And courage, the courage to bear the impact of ferocity, to bear the threat of force, to bear the prospect of death, is also something the bronze people do not wish to hear about. From the viewpoint of Jesus Christ, how are we to view those who follow the bronze dream? Today it is fashionable to be angry and indignant, to treat them as the great enemies of humanity, to scorn them as self-indulgent, self-centered, timid in the face of negatives. Such an evaluation is true, though perhaps not in a simple sense. We need to be reminded, however, that the people who follow the bronze dream do not only refuse to serve the neediness of others, they refuse to serve their own neediness. That is the pathos of their lives. The bronze people are pathetically cut off from their own essential and inescapable neediness. Therefore, they are cut off from their humanity. Neediness, after all, is the soil of all human feelings—of sharing, of love, of compassion, of humility, of courage. People who seek happiness by possessing themselves and by holding the resources for all their needs, who seek to eliminate their neediness, are sadly closed away from their own human richness.

The German poet Hans Enzensberger has written a description of the person who is smothered by possessions, who has lost all sense of himself as needy, as human. Enzensberger chooses the moment after we have dropped our coins into the cigarette machine and are standing there waiting for the cigarettes to appear, that moment when we simply wait and stare into the mirror of the vending machine.

> he puts four dimes into the slot
> he gets himself some cigarettes
>
> he gets cancer
> he gets apartheid
> he gets the king of greece
> federal tax state tax sales tax and excise
> he gets machine guns and surplus value
> free enterprise and positivism
> he gets a big lift big business big girls

the big stick the great society the big bang
the big puke
king size extra size super size

he gets more and more
for his four dimes
but for a moment all the things he is getting himself
disappear
even the cigarettes

he looks at the vending machine
but he doesn't see it
he sees himself
for a fleeting moment
and he almost looks like a man
then very soon he is gone again
with a click
there are his cigarettes

he has disappeared
it was just a fleeting moment
some kind of sudden bliss

he has disappeared
he is gone
buried under all the stuff he has gotten
for his four dimes[1]

Yet, that is not all. Those who follow the bronze dream are also cut off from love. To love requires us to have empathy for the needs of others; not only that, love requires us to be vulnerable to the suffering of others. The bronze people are those who try to hide and escape from their needs. Therefore, they are closed off from the needs of others. If need is dreadful, it is no easier to be open to it in others than in ourselves. It is the temptation of the bronze people either to ignore those who comfort them in suffering or to despise them.

Because they run from neediness the bronze people are also cut off from the God of Jesus Christ. Jesus Christ proclaims the blessedness of poverty as the necessary condition for being receptive to God's love and as the necessary condition for people's receiving and giving to one another. If you reject need, you can neither give nor receive from one another, nor receive from God. Jesus Christ establishes a celebration of neediness because neediness is indispensable for receiving—and receiving is the saying yes to love. *Receiving is the saying yes to love.*

Therefore, the bronze people who are terrified of need and who look upon poverty as the ultimate destitution cannot hear this gospel of Christ. Or if they do hear it, they find it so senseless, so perverse, as to make good what is evil, declaring that the poor are blessed in virtue of their poverty, and so they dismiss it from their minds as impossible. In Jesus Christ we are related to God as receivers, that is, in terms of our neediness. Jesus makes it clear: he comes to the poor and to the sick. Those who are well have no need of that physician. Jesus can touch no people except in relation to their continuing neediness. If we do not want to be recipients, if we cannot be one with our own neediness and therefore cannot be fully ourselves in being grateful to receive in our neediness, then Jesus will mean nothing to us. And if we want him, in meeting our needs, to remove our needs so that once having received him we require him no more, he shall disappoint us. We will take the gifts which come to us today, the gift of friendship or Christian beliefs, and try to live off those tomorrow. We will find that, like the manna in the wilderness, they will rot and stink.

BRONZE LOVE IN THE CHURCH

Such then are the ways in which the bronze dream harms the people who follow it. Yet we must face the fact that the bronze dream has penetrated the Christian faith. I am thinking especially of a common view of love which is heard in our churches, a view which reflects the bronze dream and which, while being associated with Jesus, actually rejects him. In particular, it rejects his death on the cross. By his death, Jesus makes it quite clear that the giving he exemplifies is a giving that involves giving away what we need. Not our extra time, not our surplus blood, not our unbudgeted money—Jesus has no concern for that kind of giving. Jesus in his own life exemplifies a giving that does not fear to enter into neediness, a giving away to another of what we need, so that after we have helped someone else we ourselves must call out for help and support. But, again, such giving is only possible for a people who are not frightened of being needy.

The love which is proclaimed in many churches that worship the bronze dream carefully disregards the outcome of love. These churches speak of love as helping others, but they ignore what helping others does to the person who loves. They ignore the fact that love is self-expenditure, a real expending, a real losing, a real deterioration of the self. They speak of love as if the person who is loving had no problems, had no needs. In other words, they speak of love as if the bronze dream were true! That proclamation is heard everywhere today. They say to people: "Since you have no unanswered needs, why don't you go out and help the other people who are in need?" But they never go on to add "If you do this, you too will be driven into need." By not stating the outcome of love they give the childish impression that Christian love is some kind of cornucopia where we can meet everybody's needs and problems and still have everything we need for ourselves! And believe me, there are grown-up people who speak this kind of nonsense.

There is no greater example of this bronze perversion of the Christian truth than in the common reading of the parable of the Good Samaritan. People with the bronze dream hear the parable and immediately they picture themselves as the Good Samaritan. Jesus, they think, is describing how they should be, what it means for them to love their neighbor. But in the parable, Jesus is not interested in telling us *how* to love our neighbor. The lawyer asks Jesus: *who* is my neighbor, in terms of the command that we should love our neighbor as ourselves? Jesus tells the story of the man who is robbed and beaten by thieves and who, after being neglected by the priest and Levite, is helped by the Samaritan. The Samaritan puts on oil and wine, takes the man to the inn, stays all night, and says to the inn-keeper the next day: "If you spend any more, I will repay you on my way back."

After telling this story, Jesus then repeats the lawyer's question but in terms of the story: "Which of these three . . . was neighbor to the man . . . ?" Not "Whom did the Samaritan consider to be his neighbor, whom God commands the Samaritan to love?" Of course not. The lawyer, to whom Jesus is telling the story, would not identify himself with the outcast Samaritan. But whom should the wounded man consider to be his neighbor, whom God has commanded him to love? Who proves to be a neighbor to the wounded man?

The answer is obvious: the Samaritan. We are to love the one who helps us and delivers us, who takes us to the inn, stays with us all night, and who offers to bear the full cost of our recovery. And why are we commanded to love the neighbor? Because in the realm of Jesus Christ our primary condition is need and not love. Our problem is not that we are full of love and only need Jesus to tell us to whom to direct it. That is not the human predicament. Our problem is that we are in need and have no Samaritan so to nourish us in our need that we may accept our neediness.

Who is the Good Samaritan? Who is the one who finds and helps us and bears the full cost of our recovery? The Good Samaritan is Jesus Christ. The parable concludes with Jesus' command, "Go and do as he did." But to serve our needy neighbor we are not required to fear need, to deny need, to fly from need and pretend that we are not needy. We are required, on the contrary, to recognize that *we too stand in essential poverty* just as much as any victim we try to help. Jesus could be the Good Samaritan precisely because he knew that he had nothing of his own, that he only received from the Father. Because he was one with his own neediness, he could serve those in need as their Father's representative.

But people with the bronze dream cannot possibly hear the parable in this way. They have great difficulty in identifying themselves with the wounded man. No, they prefer to see themselves as the Good Samaritan. They actually fancy themselves as being full of active love (I can't imagine why), so full of active love that they themselves will willingly bear the full cost for recovery to help another human being. (Why even a husband and wife cannot do that!) They not only fancy themselves in this way but they even ask their ministers to confirm this fancy from the pulpit.

How the words of Jesus are reoriented in the interests of wealth! As I see it, the common reading of the parable of the Good Samaritan simply imposes on the text the absurd illusion of selfless love, a one-way love—the bronze illusion that some people can give without receiving, can nourish others without thereby becoming impoverished themselves—in short, the illusion of perpetual affluence. I find no trace in Jesus of that illusion.

The dreadfulness of this illusion lies in the fact that it is so inauthentic; it is so phony. Jesus never says: "Give as if you never had any needs; give as if you were absolutely separated from the people who are needy and who seek your help." On the contrary, Jesus himself shares our needs and in this condition loves and serves. If ever you approach a needy person with the illusion that you are a creature of purely bestowing love, then to that needy person you will seem totally alien, totally superior. The lesson in Hebrews 13 is powerful: "Visit those in prison as if in prison with them! Care for the sick because you are still in the body" (Heb. 13:3, au. trans.). Active love occurs within the fellowship of neediness, within the neediness of the one who serves and leads, of the one who serves in neediness.

DEPENDENCE ON THE OTHER

Too often in our churches we hear the gospel of love without the gospel of need. Too often we hear the lie that to love is to help others without this help having any effect upon ourselves. But too often we also hear another lie: that to love our neighbors is so to give to them that they are free from need, that they too can be bronze persons. It is another lie of Christianity today, this gospel of love, this gospel which says, not that Jesus Christ enables us to be needy, but that he enables us to be loving, and by loving to remove all neediness. Christian churches today reflect such a gospel of human loving, a gospel where Jesus makes us unselfish and empowers us to nourish and sustain our needy neighbors—a gospel of the Christian spirit to remove need from the human condition.

The gospel of Jesus Christ, however, is very different. Nowhere does Jesus promise the removal of need. On the contrary, he promises to each of his followers the *intensification of need*. He calls them to take up his cross; he warns them that it is only insofar as they are willing to be poor and sick and needy that he can help them. After all, those who are healthy have no need of a physician. The only love that has anything to do with Jesus Christ is a love that has no fear of need, of neediness, of poverty. A love that is afraid of need, that wants to remove poverty, that adulates possessions and wealth—that love does not belong to those who have put on Jesus Christ.

The reason is obvious. The condition to which we are led by Jesus is a condition of *utter dependence* on God and *relative dependence* on one another. Jesus brings people to a condition where they need one another, where they call for help from one another and where they rely on one another. He does not offer a condition where people may so distribute and own commodities that they no longer have a need for one another. That is the rich person's poison—fear of need and of the needy. In Jesus Christ love thrives within need; it does not seek to remove and overcome need. No, that way of putting it is not strong enough. Love can thrive *only within* need; a love that fears need, that wants to overcome and remove need, is a lie and is therefore irrelevant. And Christian ministers that are motivated by a fear of need, by the will to remove need, and by the assumption that the minister should have no needs—such ministries can only be a torment and a shock for persons who go to them for help.

VENEER LOVE

Why is it a lie to desire to help people, in the sense of assisting them to escape from need? Because it is based on fear and because it cannot break free from fear. First, this fear of need means that when I work to help others I must not be troubled by my own neediness. I must love and help others in detachment from my own ordeal. Who can do this? Obviously bronze persons, rich people, people who are not troubled by their own need because they possess what they need. They are certainly in a position to be involved with the needs of others. And so following this model, there is an effort sometimes among us Christian ministers to possess faith in God as a basic psychic stance and to possess the power to care for others always. How treacherous! For their whole movement toward others will collapse the minute their own neediness becomes a problem.

The belief that wealth—material or psychic or spiritual—is the basis for serving our neighbor really condemns us to veneer love! At our centers, none of us feels rich. At our centers, the power of having grows very weak. If love is a matter of helping the poor from a position of strength, then that love will never be the act of a person at his or her center. It will only be part of his or her veneer. At our centers, we know that we are vulnerable and needy. For Jesus, however, vulnerability and need are exactly the conditions in which we must stand in order to love and serve. This is the message of the Hebrews 13 passage: "Care for the sick because you are still in the body." Service occurs with an acceptance of need.

Second, when love exists only to help those in need to escape from need, what does this love do when its help becomes impossible? What does the physician do when the patient is known to be dying? This love can only withdraw. This love only exists to remove need. When faced with the finality of need, with the helplessly retarded, with a terminal patient, it has no resources except to withdraw. The fundamental law of this love is: care stops where cure stops.

Third and most ironic, this love really aims for a situation where there is no more need for love and love itself can be forgotten. This love works to remove needs; when needs are removed, this love will and must disappear. But this love is not love; it is really a desire to get rid of what is unpleasant, that is, neediness. Essentially, therefore, it is unloving; essentially it is motivated by a negative reaction to need, even if that negative reaction is called love. If I can't get rid of neediness by love, well, perhaps I can get rid of neediness by ignoring it or by putting it away in institutions. If I can't get rid of suffering and need by love or by ignoring it or by putting it away in institutions, perhaps I can arrange for the needy to be killed. And so the line between love and murder begins to disappear.

I find the conduct of the United States in Vietnam to have been quite in conformity with the bronze people's kind of love, with the love that fears need above all. Vietnam became a place where American power, American self-sufficiency, American competence were tested. When our physicians can stay with the dying and can affirm them in their dying, when our parents do not condemn their children for failing, when our churches repudiate the terror of needlessness, then and only then may we condemn our politicians and our generals for trying, out of the same fear of need, to prove America's invincibility in Vietnam.

THE DANCE FROM NEED TO NEED

What is the real meaning of Christian love, when obviously Jesus expects that love to be exercised by only those who are needy, who know and accept their own neediness? What is the character of this love which only those who are constantly and joyfully grateful to God, that is, the poor, can know? The answer can be put simply. The love to which Jesus calls us is never the removal of need but *the companion of need*. Love serves need without removing need. Love does not want to give so that the other has no more use for love. Love wants to give today but only for today, so as to be able tomorrow to meet tomorrow's needs.

Even that way of putting it is not strong enough. Those who love in the name of Jesus Christ do not simply serve needs continually. No, those who love in the name of Jesus Christ serve the needs of others willingly, even to the point of being exposed in their own neediness. They begin in constant need, in which state God nourishes them. They are directed by Jesus to expend that nourishment on others and so to end in need again. And there they must ask for the help of others. It is *their need and not their love* that relates them to God and relates them to their neighbors. They do not cope with their own needs; they do not anguish over how their own needs may be met by the twists and turns of their own circumstances, by the whims of their own society, or by the stratagems of their own egos at the center of their lives, the very innermost center. They are grateful to

God because there, at the center, they let themselves be needy for God and there they do not fear their neediness. That is what frees them to serve the needy, to companion the needy, to become and be one with the needy.

Therefore, if people love in the way that Jesus Christ loves, that is, as a child of God, then they love as their way of dancing from neediness to neediness. They begin with the beseeching and they end with the beseeching when they end their activity of serving the sick or tired or defeated or demoralized or dead. They do not fear or avoid being needy; for being needy is simply how they always remain what they truly are in themselves: poor and destitute, and always ready for the nourishment of their friends, and ultimately, of their Father in heaven. Consequently, in Christian compassion and service to the weak and to the needy there can be no trace of pity. Pity is a corrupt attitude; it is expressed contempt for those who are in need, and it expresses smug superiority in those who feel it. The Christian does not nourish the poor because he or she feels sorry for them. How can he or she feel sorry for weakness and need when these are his or her own essential condition, and when these are the necessary condition for the joy of receiving?

In the United States need degrades a person; failure condemns a person, but not in the kingdom of God. To be in need is to be in a condition of honor. The needy must not be pitied but honored because they bear that condition which unites us with God, which dignifies us as children of God, and which, in that dignity, unites us to one another. Woe to the person who degrades the needy with pity. The needy are to be honored in and because of their neediness, just as Jesus is to be honored upon the cross where his destitution obtains its final form. Because we honor those in need, we nourish them as we can, letting ourselves be instruments of God's blessings and, by our service and self-expenditure, joining with them in need.

THREE MEANINGS OF DEATH

I've found the topic of death an extremely important one. I can perhaps summarize what I have been saying simply by indicating three different meanings of death. The first meaning is very prominent in the United States. Death is total obliteration, total deprivation, pure evil. Death is a kind of dreadful energy that simply destroys all good. That sense of death is related to a sense of well-being, a sense of identity by possession. I do not think the first meaning is the meaning of death in the New Testament. In the New Testament there are two different meanings of death, and it is important to distinguish them.

The second meaning is the death of which Paul speaks. Here too death simply destroys. But it destroys only in the interest of bringing forth in us a new identity. It is the death in which we join with Christ in order to be raised with Christ. In a sense, it is not a death that befalls us; what befalls us is the love and grace of God; what befalls us is a sense of the new identity. And it is out of that perception that we consent to the old identity being destroyed. In the second meaning of death, the death which Paul speaks of as dying with Christ unto sin, death is something to which we consent. It is not a fatality. We consent to it because already we have been touched by the new identity. We perceive and wish that we could be freed of the old way of being, the possessed way of being, the way of fearing all need and all dispossession. Therefore, we seek to die with Christ.

Finally and especially in the Gospel of John, there is a third meaning of death. This death is entailed in the giving of life to those who help and nourish, to those who are in need. Here there is nothing evil at all; on the contrary, this death is a *meal*. This death is a *festivity*. It is not final because God's nourishing activity continues beyond the event of death. Under this third meaning there is a sense in which the death of any person can be seen and affirmed in the perspective of love.

A CHRISTIC CELEBRATION

In conclusion, consider the Christian burial service. In that service we express our convictions about the significance of death in the light of Jesus Christ. Consider the great importance of reading an obituary, a record of the dead person's life. To the Christian, every obituary is the record of a twofold love. In reviewing the life of every person, we acknowledge how neediness has been filled by others. We indicate what has been communicated to the individual by all those who have nourished him or her. An obituary tells what the person has received by the self-expenditure of others, above all, by that of the parents and family but also by that which comes from all the anonymous ones who have sustained him or her throughout all those years. At the same time, an obituary also records this person's life, that is, the course of his or her self-expenditure in the context of his or her dying. It indicates those main arenas in which this life was slowly or quickly spilled out. In the Christic experience of the newly dead, we do not have a theophany of the absoluteness of death. We have death integrated within the rhythm of giving and receiving, within the realm of the glory in which the Father and the Son live together.

NOTE

1. Hans Magnus Enzensburger, "Vending Machine," in *Poems For People Who Don't Read Poems*, trans. Michael Hamburger, Jerome Rothenberg, and Hans Magnus Enzensburger (New York: Atheneum, 1968), 165, 167.

Afterword

So long as parents hear the screeching brakes and react with panic, they will worship death as the Lord of life.*

Arthur McGill had a gift with an image. He could horrify and haunt—simply by the choice of the apt image. He believed not in ideas, but in the orienting power of images. Ideas are abstract; we live concretely, and consequently, "we secure our sense of life and our sense of death from images." McGill intended to notice our senses for life and death. He hoped to be a theologian of the concrete, one who could root out the images by which we live. The image is central to McGill's understanding of theology.

The image of the screeching brakes certainly pained us when we first heard it. His vision of the Christian life was so impossible, so foreign, that we felt indicted for our lack of faith in a nourishing God. How little are we Americans moved by the images of Jesus to trust that God. How powerfully do images of the "bronze" people, instead, secure our sense for life and death.

This book is a study of images. McGill sets the way of Jesus, as "imaged forth" in the New Testament, alongside the images of the "bronze" life. McGill as theologian searches in our common culture for the images by which we live and with which we face death. He discovers that Americans secure their lives through the bronze people—their buoyant, succeeding, wealthy orientation. The book is also a commentary on the exploding death research of the 1970s. But McGill departs from a major premise of that research by rejecting efforts to know death better. We do not know death as an object. We cannot control it; we cannot manipulate it. We simply have no vantage point which allows us to deal with death. Ideas about death are no help; they are abstract. Even intimacy with the dying does not help us know death, much less live with death.

No trick of our minds allows us to grasp death; indeed, our thinking *dies* in death. That is, thinking is incompetent. Death mocks our ideas and our projects. Consequently, the research spawned by Elisabeth Kübler-Ross is of little help, for it worries about death exclusively as termination point. Our own termination is abstract; we are unrelated to it and only other people can know our termination.[1] No, the real death, the one we live out daily, is all our "little deaths." These McGill catalogues so powerfully as indispensable images "in which the truth about life and death seems to be disclosed to us."

As critic, McGill seeks to free us from images which bring us to despair (the panic of the screeching brakes). He turns us to the newspapers, to the arts, literature, and advertising of our times. By gentle ridicule and with a sense of irony, he forces us to objectify and name our images. We may be shocked; we may get defensive. But McGill continues to hammer away. His diagnosis of American culture and its version of the Christian gospel leaves little or no room for anyone to escape judgment.

We participate in death. We are insiders to it. If we can see the despair our images bring us, possibly we can be ready to find other images more primitive, more realistic, more humane. These McGill finds in the New Testament. In his view theology is a pilgrimage out of despair toward courage under the power of images which create possibility.

For McGill theology is a pilgrimage toward the light which transfigures existence. He embraces a classic method, yet one out of step with many recent discussions. In fact, he refuses to take up the question of method in abstraction.[2] Theology presupposes the pilgrimage and contributes directly to it. If theology is to be redemptive, it always arises from and returns to "our existence itself in its questionableness."[3] What is the meaning of violence? In what are we dispossessed? Why is the Christmas child crucified?

The theologian wants, works for, and waits upon the disclosure of the divine light. Revelation is the conferring of the divine life onto those who wait in need.[4] While theology always presupposes revelation, it actually enhances the light through an event of understanding. Here McGill stands within the faith-seeking-understanding pattern for theology, but especially in a way reminiscent of Karl Barth.[5] Theology is not centrally critical reflection on revelation, nor simply the work of professional academicians, but the midwife in the lived transition from darkness to light.

McGill's model for theology inspires a specific approach to biblical texts. He will not be bound by the strictures of historical criticism when he exegetes the Bible. Those trained as historical and textual critics may wince at his exegetical freedom. For instance, he has no interest in the "historical" Jesus. That Jesus, McGill suspects, is one more strategy of modern death denial.[6] Rather, his interest is in the New Testament images of Jesus which call us out of our darkness. He seeks an almost pneumatic release of the power latent in a set of images.[7]

In order for us to sense the possibility that these New Testament images provide, McGill must first unmask the images which Americans find powerful. The first two chapters contain a description (a phenomenology) of the bronze life, painful to any American reader. Instead of a disclosure of light, the world appears darker, existence more questionable. McGill presses on. He does not see the punishing judgment of God, but the preliminary disclosure of God's light, a first moment of God's transfiguration of human existence.

Theology cannot make the disclosure happen, even though human understanding participates in the transfiguration of life. "A theological method tells us the *conditions* in which the event of understanding seems likely to occur (though not necessarily and not automatically)."[8] The theologian cannot guarantee the event of revelation, as if it depends only on some correct interpretation of the Bible or on some right method. God does not give light to humans in such a way that it can be possessed and packaged. No, the theologian gets ready and waits as a receiver.

McGill's point on method reflects his concern to include the intellect within human sinfulness. For McGill sin does not take hold in one errant part of the human, such as in the will. Rather, it invades the constitution of the "I" itself—the identity of the self out of which the self acts. Every aspect of the human participates in a sinful drive to possess and control the world and, especially, the identity of the self. The mind too would possess itself. It would grasp and contain God's Word. McGill's view of sin requires that we adapt our theology to the critique of possessed identity. This critique reminds theology of its neediness by insisting upon an Augustinian moment of illumination. Not our theology, not our methods, not even our faith can secure our identities as an enduring possession. Theologians, then, do not escape human dependence on God. Every day, human understanding is every bit as needy of fresh, clear insight as is the stomach of food.

Consequently, theologians must enter into the questions and answers of a culture. They have to develop an ear for the concrete, sensuous language of existence, not simply to speak the vernacular in order to be understood, but to enter into the condition of "flesh," the mortal and essentially needy condition of being human. Only in concrete experience does theology find the data on which it works. Only there will it remember its own poverty.

In *The Celebration of Flesh*, a study of poetry in the Christian life, McGill speaks of the "shock" of ordinary experience. Experience often triggers flight or avoidance. Avoidance becomes a spiritual problem for "viewpoint Christianity," as McGill calls it. Viewpoint Christianity attempts a static world view which Christians use as a buffer against shock. Viewpoint Christianity, whether consciously or not, draws into it a technical theology to close itself to the world. Technical theology always conspires to create an orthodoxy, in the worst sense of the term. Once an orthodoxy is in place, Christians cannot hear of God's openness to the world.

Poetry can break apart an orthodoxy and reacquaint it with the fleshly and needy condition of being human. Usually, however, theologians employ poets as the voices which portray the modern human predicament. They favor those who describe the disaster of modernity, who set the problem. Then they present the message which meets the modern cry of agony. But McGill will not understand the poet simply as a poser of our questions. Rather, McGill insists that Christians should value poets not for their visions of the world or for the questions they ask, but precisely because they suspend judgments and simply notice the world with immediacy. For McGill the issue is not whether the poetic litany of despair is true, but whether we will let poets describe a level of experience that we overlook. Will we let them shock us? Poets engage in the flesh—the medium through which we meet the world and God. Far from distracting from the Christian life, poetry can be enjoyed simply for its celebration of the flesh, simply as a visceral engagement with the world. Poetry, read in this way, can check spiritual pride and alienation from the flesh.

When McGill turns to the poet's images or to the flash of a newspaper headline, he follows the dictates of a phenomenologist who wants to discern the way life and death *appear*. Appearances are the primary data on which reflection works. Once McGill chronicles the unfolding of lived experience, he applies a normative step. That is, he pushes his phenomenology into a complex correlation with other images. He wants both to evaluate whether the bronze life is realistic to the given terms of the world and to open that life to the possibility of "transfiguration." The bronze life tests out poorly because it refuses to believe that human life is *mortal*. So far as it pursues patterns of avoidance, it closes itself to a possible metamorphosis into divine light. It can only view suffering and death as utterly anti-human, as demonic. Before this power bronze life ends finally in despair.

Theology needs to be open to the shocks of existence; indeed, it must recreate the shocks. McGill's theology is shocking. He pokes at carefully protected soft spots and will not let us rest under the power of demonic images of death. He shows our images to be the construction of a false consciousness. Then he jars us with alternative, transfiguring images in which death is desacralized in Christ. We get a hint that mortal life is within our reach. He appeals to older loyalties, to times and ways before life came so dressed up. He elicits intuitions deeper than bronze, which hold a memory of our mortality. The active work of theology opens a way for the possibility of voicing God's answer to the human plea for redemption. However, God's redeeming activity brings *no end* to the neediness in which we suffer and die. Redemption transforms people so that they can *bear* the negative.

We must speak more fully of the transfiguration McGill has in mind. Death seldom stands in the center of Christian theology any more. At best it is a sideshow which we note only when it cannot be avoided—at funerals. Even then, death is hidden behind the mortician's craft and sermons on immortality. McGill, however, thinks that death is the most conspicuous feature of Christian existence. The death of Jesus on a cross stands as the visible image of revelation and redemption. The central sacraments of Baptism and Eucharist celebrate a focus on death. Consequently, when McGill sets out to lecture on death, he really has to sketch in miniature a systematic theology.

McGill certainly wants to transform our views on death. But his contribution goes well beyond the many voices which point to the American denial of death, voices which do not tackle the fundamental religious issue. Siding with his colleague William F. May and the phenomenological research of van der Leeuw, McGill uncovers the essential sacral character of our views of death.[9] Death is our taboo. We exhibit both a revulsion which drives us from any trace of death and an uncanny attraction to it. Because we hold death as taboo, because in so doing we sacralize death, McGill insists we must approach our images of life and death through the theme of *worship*. Whom or what do we take to be the final reality with which we must deal? Whom or what do we worship?

With his sacral diagnosis of death, McGill obviously rejects the idea that modern life has been secularized. Instead, McGill discerns a disenchantment with one cult and a subtle replacement by another. Indeed, the modern apathetic world is wildly religious, dominated by an absolute Lord. When we Americans commit ourselves to resisting and avoiding the negative at all cost, we are simply responding worshipfully to what we take to be determinative of our lives. At a deep and despairing level we know that death wins. Were we to be dislodged from that persuasion, we would have to be convinced that the absolute, created in our taboo, is not, in fact, absolute. We would have to sense the pull of some other power amid our neediness. Jesus, according to McGill, desacralizes death, and thus opposes divinity as we understand it. Jesus poses a religious attack on religion.

McGill's constructive theology turns on an understanding of human neediness. Behind the conspicuous theme of death stands the religious problem of neediness. Neediness unifies all the little deaths we die. Neediness founds Christian relationships to self, to neighbor, to God, and is the flavor of Christian love. Fear of neediness, on the contrary, is the precondition of human sinfulness and is the real evil which stands behind the denial of death. Theology must discover how we handle neediness. McGill shows that everything American goes away from need and that everything Christian goes toward need. If McGill is right, then American sensibilities require radical transformation: we must learn to accept neediness. Accepting neediness is a grace which can empower people with courage in the face of need.

Human need always outstrips our resources, no matter what we do to secure enough "wealth" to protect ourselves. Just when we "have it made," we experience the actual or possible dissolution of that achievement. One or more dimensions of our lives are *always* insecure. In this discrepancy between our needs and what resources can deliver, we suffer. For McGill everyone suffers and always suffers. Everyone is in need. Americans, however, construe need as *evil*. Need-as-evil energizes their ethic of avoidance and resistance. They run from horror into an imaginary world they half-know to be illusory. In the face of the unthinkable—that their lives whirl out of control—they galvanize all resources to resist need. Eventually resistance runs aground and turns into a larger passion to camouflage the negatives of life, a passion to secure an artistic triumph over what offends them deeply.

Once we note the dual American ethic, we can see the problem posed by death. Death is unrelieved neediness, the final fruit of all the needs which show their faces every day. The American denial of death is simply the most evident element of a systematic avoidance of need in our culture. All our attitudes toward life are informed by this project. McGill understands that every human faces a primal choice before the condition of need: either to run from need or to rest in need. The former choice is the condition of sin; the latter, the condition of salvation.[10]

A culture which systematically avoids need pushes death to the end of life. Obviously McGill rejects the American tendency to fix death as termination point. Death as termination is an abstraction constructed analogically from our daily experiences of "little deaths." Americans project the state of unrelieved need upon the end of life and thereby separate themselves from the marks of death. They retreat into a shell of a life, where they neither nourish others nor are nourished by others. Consequently, the cost of flight is a profound alienation from life.

Not only do bronze people slide into a way of being which opposes Christian life, they lose touch with a primitive truth of nature: life lives by consuming life. That is, life depends on mutual nourishment. It starts in need, thrives when it needs, reaches out for what others need, and passes on what it takes to others in need. Neediness and nourishment are the two faces of the death which daily constitutes life. Bronze people, however,

will have none of this ecology. They look at the natural cycle of consump-
tion and see only the slaughter bench of history. Ironically, their well-
meaning horror at the negative generates an anti-human project.

The images of Jesus present a possible transfiguration of that project.
They offer life, but only in and amid death. The "kingdom of God" is a
power to communicate life but only in the "eating" of life. Naturally, the
sharing of life in the kingdom contradicts the absolute terror of dispossession which drives American life. These two responses to neediness presup-
pose different understandings of how humans constitute their identities.
The bronze person seeks an identity without need through the "technique of having." The demand for security requires that people insulate
themselves from every hint of neediness, from attachments to other people, and, ultimately, from the worship of God. In short, bronze people die
in their escape from death.

In Jesus identity becomes decentered or "ecstatic." One moment, a person lives insofar as he or she stands empty, without resources, ready to
receive nourishment from others. The next, a person lives insofar as he or
she gives away the very resources needed for life. McGill speaks of the new
identity in Jesus as an "ecstatic identity," that is, as an identity constituted
by a standing-outside-of-the-self. McGill traces it exegetically in three relations: to the self, to the neighbor, and to God. When we decide how we
constitute our identities, whether in the resources we can possess or in the
needs which cry out beyond us, we decide whether we live in sin or in the
divine light. Jesus' experience as the one "from the Father" authorizes the
way which lives from beyond the self. Jesus *is*, not in himself, but as he
receives himself and only as he gives himself away. Never simply an "I,"
Jesus lives absolutely dependent on God and relatively dependent on others. Need pervades his identity, and he lives by entering death.

To be transformed into an identity constituted by death, we would have
to do the impossible: mimic Jesus' *choosing* to die. It would take courage.
But the steps are already charted before us and, perhaps, dimly known.
When we tire of flight, we may be ready for another way. When flight is
simply not possible, we may find that even the way of death is possible. An
ecstatic identity can recast the sacral meaning of death. If we can enter
death, then death is not the awesome dominator we imagine. Entering
need does not exterminate us, as we fear. It brings life. If we were to make
a career of need and die fully, we would be maximally alive.

McGill's critique of possessed identity informs his interpretation of New Testament eschatological symbols. According to the New Testament, powers that dominate and destroy life do not prevail. "Resurrection," a life in need and self-expenditure, affirms that nothing cuts humans off from the nourishing of others and, finally, of God. McGill's move is subtle. If one receives one's self and makes that very self available for others to receive, then emptiness is not a measure of loss but of gain. People are full, maximally alive when they have expended themselves fully for others. "Resurrection" designates the ironic inversion of identity when humans discover that they are related to others and to God only by way of need. There is no end to need, even in heaven, for we shall always need the nourishing love which comes from beyond us and shall always be called to nourish others in need.

With the help of the Gospel of John, especially, McGill recovers a shocking Christian idea. Life is never anything we *have*. It is never a possession, never something given over to us. If we never have life, then we never escape need. We always reach out, dependent on others and on God to nourish us in our poverty. And if we never possess anything, we have nothing to hold back from others who need. Jesus images forth this more primitive definition of life. Life is no quality or essence owned by a person. Life is the passing on of life, the feeding of life with life. Similarly, divine life is the communication of life, the contagion of self-giving from the Father to the Son (who stand in need of each other) and, by extension, to those empty ones who receive Jesus' received identity when he turns it over to his people waiting at the cross. For McGill divine life and human life can be continuous; he finds the warrant for this continuity in the Athanasian doctrine of the Trinity. Athanasius views the Trinity as the doctrine which protects an understanding of God as an engendering divinity. God is God because the Father gives over the divine life to the Son who in turn shares it with humanity.

McGill's book ends with a vision of Christian love as the sharing of divine life. As critic, McGill exposes the loneliness and alienation of the closed system of the bronze people. Even when they try to love, they do so under the illusion that love does not need. American love proceeds from wealth, from having. It is essentially philanthropic, in the sense that it moves from strength to weakness and seeks to bring the weak to strength. McGill finds this American orientation unrealistic and a perversion of

Christian love. If neediness never ends and neediness conditions our relationship to the self, to neighbor, and to God, then there can be no room
for sharing surpluses in Christian love. Love costs dearly and the expression of love cannot hope to move people into a state of affluence. Christian
love does not hold back what it needs to live, and it should not seek to
remove need; rather, Christian love is a dynamic sharing, a giving and
receiving.

These are, perhaps, troubling ideas in an age dominated by demands for
liberation. Actually, McGill's ideas do contribute to the current discussion
in at least two respects. First, he offers a clear, if controversial, criterion by
which service can be identified as distinctly Christian. Love is Christian
love when it expends the self so that the self moves into greater need and
requires the love of God and others in return. Indeed, Christian love drives
others into need so that they too will reach out for help. McGill, then,
offers a radical vision of the self as social. Its primary object is the sharing
of need. Since McGill will not give up on love as self-expenditure, his
ethics reject any vision of liberation that implies individualism or defines
human freedom as needlessness. Such liberation, for McGill, would be
only a new form of death-denial, launching new forms of oppression.

Second, McGill's critique of possessed identity helps us understand
why we dominate others. By locating our possessiveness in the decision
we make to constitute our identities, McGill uncovers the power which
defines our lives. Most Americans find themselves in a life-and-death
struggle with evil defined very differently from that presupposed by liberation theologies. Their apathy arises not from insensitivity or greed, but
from the way that death offends them deeply. McGill's analysis teaches us
why prophetic demands for liberation so often fall on deaf ears: Americans are already consumed by a struggle for liberation from the negative
defined as need. They dutifully live within a sacral drama which requires
acts of possession and a fictive sleight of hand.

Common critiques of American wealth do not appreciate the precise
sacral significance of the fetishes and ideologies of the bronze person.
Consequently, these critiques come off as world and wealth hating. They
motivate us by guilt and hatred of the things of the world. McGill will have
none of this. The question of evil does not turn on what we have, our
possessions, but on the manner in which we constitute our identities.
Things of the world are a sign of God's shared blessing, if we constitute

ourselves in need. To an age dominated by demands for liberation, then, McGill offers an analysis of why we cannot bear to love and a description of what would have to happen for us to hear and respond to the charge to serve the neighbor.

PER M. ANDERSON
CHARLES A. WILSON
May 1986

NOTES

* Remarks by Arthur C. McGill at the Annual Meeting of the American Academy of Religion (= AAR), Chicago, October 1975.

1. In the first chapter McGill distinguishes between a popular understanding and a medical understanding of death. The two overlap somewhat in that they both view death as obliteration; however, while the medical view fixes on the narrow sense of death as termination of life, the popular understanding is haunted by the continual experience of dying. See also McGill's introduction.

2. Arthur C. McGill, *Suffering: A Test of Theological Method* (Philadelphia: Geneva Press, 1968, repr.; Philadelphia: Westminster Press, 1982), chaps. 1 and 8. See also idem, *The Celebration of Flesh: Poetry in Christian Life* (New York: Associated Press, 1964), chap. 1.

3. *Suffering,* 122.

4. As suggested below, McGill is very serious about God's presence in understanding. This insight redeems humanity as an experience of power. Here McGill takes up Gerardus van der Leeuw's conviction that the sacred is disclosed as power. Throughout *Suffering,* the category of power predominates. In this volume, the dynamic of giving and receiving is a power relationship. Receptivity is, for McGill, a form of power. He believes that John wants to elevate Jesus' receiving from a subordinate position in relation to giving. God the Father and God the Son are equal in power. This means that human dependence upon and thirst for God's power need not be construed as selfishness. Rather, human relationships with God depend upon this receptivity. See van der Leeuw's *Religion in Essence and Manifestation.*

5. Cf. McGill's important essay, "Recent Discussions of Anselm's Argument," in the anthology on Anselm's argument for God which McGill and John Hick edited: *The Many-Faced Argument* (New York: Macmillan, 1967), 33–110.

6. The AAR speech of October 1975 (Chicago) addressed the way in which physicians, morticians, and historians function professionally within the expectations of a death-denying culture. McGill's remarks concerning history writing as a strategy of death-denial were especially keen.

7. Many who heard these lectures in 1974 charged McGill with an exegetical

and hermeneutical naivete. Indeed, he showed little interest in reconstructing an original version of a text; he would not be held to the law of authorial intention; he vaulted over the historical reconstruction of Jesus' life and message. Since the 1970s, however, certain developments in hermeneutics vindicate his approach considerably. In fact, the text is more hermeneutically nuanced than it seems. Actually, it works with a sophisticated mutual correlation between the problem (set in the American images) and the solution (seen in the New Testament images of Jesus).

8. *Suffering*, 123.

9. Remarks at the AAR meeting October 1975. Cf. William F. May, "The Sacral Power of Death in Contemporary Experience," *Social Research* 39 (Fall 1972): 463–88; and van der Leeuw, *Religion in Essence and Manifestation.*

10. In these chapters, the evil of sin stands out over the priority of the demonic in *Suffering.* For McGill the demonic is widely felt today as the experience of violent, destructive power. Clearly, he wishes to distinguish the demonic from the evil of sin. But in the third chapter, McGill does suggest a characteristic common to the demonic and sin. Evil in the broadest sense is the power of domination. Horror over need makes Americans particularly vulnerable to dominating power and naturally inclined to participate in domination through the technique of having.

ACKNOWLEDGMENTS

"Blue Girls" by John Crowe Ransom. Copyright 1927 by Alfred A. Knopf, Inc. and renewed 1955 by John Crowe Ransom. Reprinted from *Selected Poems, Third Edition, Revised and Enlarged*, by John Crowe Ransom, by permission of Alfred A. Knopf, Inc. and Methuen, London, Ltd.

Catch 22 by Joseph Heller. Copyright © 1955, 1961 by Joseph Heller. Reprinted by permission of Simon & Schuster, Inc. and Jonathan Cape, Ltd.

"American Rhapsody" by Kenneth Fearing in *New and Selected Poems* by Kenneth Fearing. Reprinted by permission of the publisher, Indiana University Press.

Ulysses by James Joyce. Copyright 1942, 1946 by Nora Joseph Joyce. Copyright 1934 by the Modern Library Inc. Copyright renewed 1961 by Lucia and George Joyce. Reprinted by permission of the publisher, Random House.

"The Convergence of the Twain" from *The Complete Poems of Thomas Hardy* edited by James Gibson. Reprinted by permission of Macmillan Publishing Co., Inc.

The Plague by Albert Camus, translated by Stuart Gilbert. Copyright 1948 by Stuart Gilbert. Reprinted by permission of the publisher, Random House.

Excerpts from *Basic Writings of Nietzsche*, translated and edited, with commentaries, by Walter Kauffmann. Reprinted by permission of the publisher, Random House.

Hans Magnus Enzensburger, "Vending Machine" from *Poems for People Who Don't Read Poems*. Copyright © 1967 by Hans Magnus Enzensburger. Reprinted with the permission of Atheneum Publishers, Inc., and Martin Secker & Warburg, Ltd.